HAPPY AT WORK

Prentice Hall LIFE

If life is what you make it, then making it better starts here.

What we learn today can change our lives tomorrow. It can change our goals or change our minds; open up new opportunities or simply inspire us to make a difference. That's why we have created a new breed of books that do more to help you make more of *your* life.

Whether you want more confidence or less stress, a new skill or a different perspective, we've designed *Prentice Hall Life* books to help you to make a change for the better. Together with our authors we share a commitment to bring you the brightest ideas and best ways to manage your life, work and wealth.

In these pages we hope you'll find the ideas you need for the life *you* want. Go on, help yourself.

It's what you make it

* * *

HAPPY AT WORK

Ten steps to ultimate job satisfaction

Sophie Rowan

Harlow, England • London • New York • Boston • San Francisco • Toronto • Sydney • Singapore • Hong Kong
Tokyo • Seoul • Taipei • New Delhi • Cape Town • Madrid • Mexico City • Amsterdam • Munich • Paris • Milan

Pearson Education Limited

Edinburgh Gate
Harlow CM20 2JE
Tel: +44 (0)1279 623623
Fax: +44 (0)1279 431059
Website: www.pearsoned.co.uk

First published in Great Britain in 2008

ISBN: 978-0-273-71423-1

British Library Cataloguing-in-Publication Data
A catalogue record for this book is available from the British Library.

Library of Congress Cataloging-in-Publication Data
Rowan, Sophie.
    Happy at work : ten steps to ultimate job satisfaction / Sophie Rowan.
        p. cm.
    Includes bibliographical references and index.
    ISBN-13: 978-0-273-71423-1 (pbk.)
1. Job satisfaction. 2. Quality of work life. I. Title.
    HF5549. 5. J63R637 2008
    650. 1–dc22

                                                          2007041897

10 9 8 7 6 5 4 3 2 1
11 10 09 08 07

Cartoons by Bill Piggins

Typeset in 10/15pt IowanOldSt BT by 3

Printed in Great Britain by Henry Ling Ltd., at the Dorset Press, Dorchester, Dorset

The Publishers' policy is to use paper manufactured from sustainable forests.

For Alan

CONTENTS

ACKNOW-
LEDGEMENTS

Happy at Work was a team effort, and resulted from the guidance, collaboration and support of the following people. The team at Pearson, especially my editors Samantha Jackson and Elizabeth Rix provided unstinting support throughout. My business partners, John Deely and Elaine Nicholls, whose support and friendship have always been more than generous. Nikki Walsh, editor of my careers column, was a constant source of guidance. A big thank-you also to Vanessa Harriss who edited early drafts of Happy at Work; researcher Yseult Freaney; illustrators Richard Slator and Bill Piggins; my lawyer Geraldine East and Bella Saer who helped me enormously with the proposal.

My family was hugely supportive throughout. My parents, Kathleen and Fergus, provided me with the perfect writing space and mint tea on tap. My four fabulous sisters read draft after draft and provided invaluable feedback. Anna and Eve played an absolute blinder. My friends provided me with great encouragement, especially Michelle Hegarty and Orla Keenan.

Genuine thanks to the many colleagues, clients, associates and mentors I consulted in relation to this book, especially those who featured in the case studies; you are too numerous to mention but thank you so much for sharing your knowledge, experience and insights with me. Dr Martyn Newman and Siobhan Hamilton-Phillips read 'Happy at Work' prior to publication and I am most appreciative of their generous feedback.

I am grateful to the pioneers in the field of positive psychology and beyond who kindly allowed me to use their material or to represent their ideas. Dr Martin Seligman; Dr Stephen Covey; The Hogans and Geoff Trickey at Psychological Consultancy Ltd; Chartered Institute of Personnel Development; and healthyplace.com.

In some instances, we have been unable to trace the owners of copyright material and we would appreciate any information that would enable us to do so.

ABOUT THE AUTHOR

Sophie Rowan is an Occupational Psychologist with almost 15 years' experience working in the field of Career Development and Coaching. For the past six years, she has worked as a partner for Dublin-based business psychologists, Pinpoint. Pinpoint, (www.pinpoint.ie) is a niche consultancy in Dublin that helps companies choose and develop the best talent, and helps individuals to get the most out of their career. Previous to that she was Head of Career Development at Career Psychology Ltd. London.

Sophie is an active member of both the Psychological Society of Ireland (PSI) and the British Psychological Society (BPS) and has been involved with press and media affairs on a voluntary basis for both organisations over the past 10 years. Through her involvement with PSI, she helped organise 2 national careers events for undergraduate psychology students and has spoken at a number of Careers Fairs on her area of expertise, Occupational Psychology.

Sophie writes regular careers features for a number of publications and was careers columnist for Prudence magazine for the past 2 years. Whilst working in London, Sophie was the in-house careers expert for i–circle.com and wrote regularly for the national press.

Sophie lives in Dublin with her husband Alan.

INTRODUCTION

Why *Happy at Work?*

Work takes up about half of your day, so choosing a job that makes you happy is very important. Yet, about 25 per cent of workers spend their work life feeling unsatisfied with their lot. That's one in every four people who really don't like going to work every day.

Any of the following situations ring a bell?

- Stuck in a rut?
- Feel sick on Sundays; can't face Mondays?

- Spend your time day-dreaming about your ideal job?
- Lost your confidence?
- Feel invisible or overlooked?
- Can't stand your boss or colleague?
- Can't stand up to your boss or colleague?
- Working too hard, can't switch off?

Well, join the club. The fact is that none of us will get through our career without experiencing some type of career blip. Job dissatisfaction doesn't just affect your job – it affects your whole life, so it makes sense to tackle these situations head-on. One or more of the above *will* happen to you at some point in your career. What's important is how you deal with these situations when they arise. Rest assured that there are a number of solutions to all of the above. *Happy at Work* will show you how to work through these situations to make your work life the best it can be.

What is happiness?

One thing that all happiness experts agree on is that happiness is not a destination. Rather, it is the result of a range of activities and feelings. Or to use that rather corny phrase, happiness is a journey.

So, what is the key to being happy at work?

Let's go right back to basics here. If you're too busy, too stressed or simply dissatisfied, it's all too easy to overlook the obvious. In order to have a happy work life, you need to:

1 Do something you like doing

2 Do something that suits your personality and work style

3 Do it well *and*

4 Treat people well.

Simple as that. Do those four things consistently throughout your career and you are likely to have a pretty good time at work. Well that's the theory anyway. The reality is that, from time to time, situations arise that cause unhappiness. There are times where you have no control over these events. Say your company axes flexi-working so you're now stuck in rush hour traffic; or you get the boss from hell. But often times, you *do* have control over the things that make you unhappy. Not getting on well with a colleague or a boss, suffering from lack of confidence, not feeling that you 'fit' in your team of company. These are all things that you can fix or improve. Maybe you just don't know how. And this is where *Happy at Work* comes in – common-sense advice that is easy to apply to your own work situation.

How will *Happy at Work* help you?

This book will change your working life and make it more manageable and more pleasant. You will achieve this by doing the following two things:

1 Tackle or remove the things that make you unhappy

2 Identify the things that make you happy and learn to actively pursue them.

Doing this in a step-by-step manner, where you build on your experience and confidence as you go, is actually easier than you might think.

In *Happy at Work*, each step deals with a particular theme. You'll explore everyday work situations that relate to that theme. There are lots of practical and user-friendly solutions to common workplace problems. For example, Step 4 is all about communication, and it's packed full of tips and techniques that will help you get on better with your colleagues.

The three happiness themes

Happy at Work is divided into three sections. Section 1 is called **Managing Yourself** and helps you identify and explore what makes YOU happy at work. Section 2 is all about **Managing Others** and tells you how to make the most of your work relationships. And Section 3, **Managing Your World of Work**, describes how to create the best opportunities for yourself.

This book will provide practical and user-friendly advice about what helps or hinders your work happiness. You'll find workable solutions that minimise your happiness hindrances and maximise your happiness helpers!

All of the advice contained in *Happy at Work* is backed up by the latest research from top career psychologists. It's also full of real-life career stories and draws on my clients' experiences of making real improvements to their work life. Simple quick-fixes, mantras and workplace tips are presented alongside tables of workable solutions that encourage you to apply the

advice to your own situation. And finally, there are some great questions included in each Step to get you thinking further about your own situation.

And remember, an ounce of practice is worth more than a ton of theory. Reading this book is a great starting point but to get real value, put the advice into action and watch your happiness grow.

Good luck and enjoy ☺

"

Happiness is the meaning and the purpose of life, the whole aim and end of human existence.

Aristotle

"

MANAGING YOURSELF

Section 01

STEP 1	Know yourself
STEP 2	Choose to be happy
STEP 3	Your happiness plan

Working as a psychologist in the area of career development, I meet many people who are unhappy in their careers. Many of them talk about drifting into an unsuitable situation almost without realising it, and finding themselves still stuck there some years later. They speak about their situation almost as if their career has happened to them and they are looking in from the outside, whereas the reality is that *you* are the central character in your career – and what happens in your career is primarily determined by you.

The first thing that becomes evident in these conversations is that we often underestimate how powerful we can be as people, and this leads to us putting up with unacceptable situations. One of the key messages of this book is that you *can* change unacceptable situations – it's not always easy, but there is always a way. I believe that reading this book, and putting into practice what you read, will prove this.

Section 1 'Managing Yourself' includes Steps 1 to 3. In Step 1, you start your journey to a happier you by taking a long hard look at yourself and your own situation. Building your self-awareness is key to highlighting the things that make you happy (and unhappy) and this sets the scene for Step 2.

In Step 2 you will learn about the importance of your *attitude* to change. Choosing to be happier is a good starting point in actively pursuing what makes you happy. You'll take a realistic view of what may be holding you back. You'll also look at practical ways to overcome the obstacles that stand in the way of your happiness.

That brings us to Step 3, which will show you how to apply this understanding to your own situation. Knowing about yourself is one thing, but actively using that information to enhance your situation is another. In Step 3 you'll look at making new happiness habits a permanent fixture in your work life. This section concludes by looking at the concrete ways in which to keep your happiness on track.

"What we do belongs to what we are; and what we are is what becomes of us."

Henry Van Dyke, US author

and academic

Know yourself

01

Let's start at the very beginning and embark on Step 1 with a good look at what career satisfaction actually means.

Satisfaction saturation point?

Through my work, I meet lots of people who are unhappy at work. I can generally place them in one of two categories. The first are those who are unhappy because of a genuine mismatch between them as a person and the career they have chosen. The second are those who have chosen their career path well but are still unhappy. In many cases, they have been happy up to a certain point but have reached what I call their 'satisfaction saturation point'. This is the point where a career that was once fulfilling and exciting has over time become dull, routine or unsatisfactory. Sounds familiar? Yes, we have all been there. Generally, your first response when this happens is to assume that you're in the wrong career, which leaves you with little option but to

1 change career *or*
2 stay put, but resign yourself to a less than fulfilling career.

Choose the right option

Sometimes a career change is indeed the preferable option. But what if it's not a feasible option for you? What if you can't afford to re-train, take a salary cut, or spend ten years getting to the same level you're at in a different career? And what if you're not actually in the wrong career, but you've simply forgotten to take notice of the things you actually enjoy? Does that automatically mean counting down the days to your pension in misery? Thankfully, *no*.

There is a third and far less stressful option. That is, do what you can to improve your lot, and create the best and happiest work situation for yourself in the process. How to do this? Read on. Just follow the advice given, apply it to your own situation and you *will* be happier at work.

Self-awareness

Happiness at work starts with self-awareness. And what is self-awareness? It's defined as the act of 'focusing attention on oneself'. In other words, keeping an eye on how things are going for you. Why is this important for being happier at work? Well, research tells us that those who are self-aware have a clearer sense of where they want to be and how to get there. And self-aware people take more responsibility for their behaviour. These are all important parts of improving your job satisfaction.

It has also been linked to improved communication and, as you'll see in Steps 4 to 7, how you communicate with others has a strong impact on your work happiness. Self-aware people are more inclined to identify the things in their lives that need

HAPPINESS AT WORK STARTS WITH SELF-AWARENESS

change or improvement. And finally, they are more likely to improve themselves through self-enhancement. That's really what this book is about: enhancing your work life and increasing your happiness.

So, the case for self-awareness is strong. It's clear to see why increased self-awareness is an important factor in your work happiness.

How to build your self-awareness

The key question is: how do you become more self-aware? Looking at your work happiness, three things are crucial:

- Learn from experience
- Reflect on where you are now
- Identify what's important to you in your career.

Charting your career satisfaction

Looking back at what has made you happy in the past is the best way to predict what will make you happy in the future.

Look at the graph opposite.

This is a picture of what most people experience in their career – some career highs, some career lows and maybe a career change at some point.

The very fortunate amongst you haven't experienced as many (or any) career troughs as above, so congratulations! No doubt you have chosen your career path well and have worked hard to

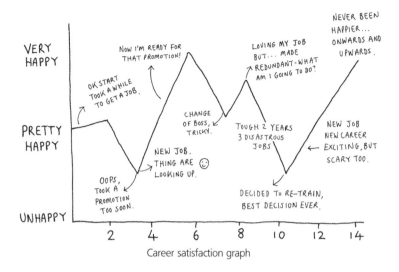

Career satisfaction graph

forge a happy work life. More likely (if you're reading this book) you haven't experienced as many career highs as you'd like and there is no time like the present to address that situation. From today, you are working towards a happier work future and, believe it or not, just the process of reading this book is getting you closer to making that happen for yourself.

Whatever your situation, mapping out your own career satisfaction graph is an important step in uncovering the trends and patterns that have occurred in your career to date. Take time to focus on your own situation and what you want from your work life. This should become a regular part of your work routine, something that you undertake every six months or so.

Here's my career satisfaction graph and what I learned from it.

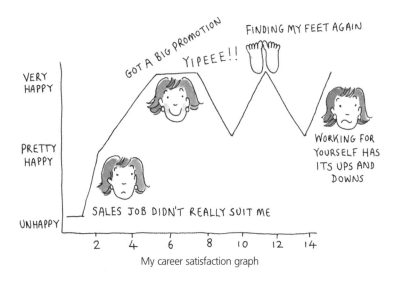

VERY HAPPY

PRETTY HAPPY

UNHAPPY

GOT A BIG PROMOTION

YIPEEE!!

FINDING MY FEET AGAIN

WORKING FOR YOURSELF HAS ITS UPS AND DOWNS

SALES JOB DIDN'T REALLY SUIT ME

2 4 6 8 10 12 14

My career satisfaction graph

My Story: Career Highs and Lows

My first foray into the world of work or my 'career' was less than fulfilling – I managed to start my work life in completely the wrong career! After completing my degree in pure psychology at University College Dublin, I spent a fantastic gap year in Italy working in bars and restaurants, having the time of my life. That life had a very clear end point, however, and much as I loved Italy, I knew that sadly, my career did not lie in the hospitality industry in Bologna. I was at a loss as to what to do when I returned home to Ireland. This was the early 1990s and the Celtic Tiger hadn't quite arrived on our shores. I enrolled on a course in Marketing and Advertising, because it fitted my very broad objective of working in an area that involved people and business. The dramatic 'Unhappy' at the start of the chart signals my first 'career crisis' very early in my career.

After the course I secured a job placement in the Ad department of a national newspaper, selling advertising space. Despite being absolutely miserable and clearly not very good in this field, I was offered a job on a commission-only basis after my placement – and took it! This was not a good time for me. I am a very poor sales person if I don't believe in the product. I am not motivated by money (although I fret if I can't pay the bills). And I hate talking on the phone in front of other people. And there I was in an open plan office, cold-calling businesses, selling very little ad space, so no commission – disastrous! Needless to say, that job didn't last long.

A family event in London created my next opportunity. I looked up an old college friend who was working for a careers consultancy. They had an opportunity for psychology a graduate trainee, which she put me forward for, and I got the job. The seven years I spent in London working in Career Psychology were very happy ones for me. This was a small company with a solid reputation in bespoke career development programmes. It was run by a very warm and charismatic boss and there was a great team of people involved. I was given lots of responsibility and autonomy from early on. Within five years I had become Head of Career Development and had completed my Masters in Occupational Psychology through part-time study.

This was a really exciting time for me. I worked hard and gave the job my all. In my last two years at CPL, I was seeing 10–12 clients a week for full careers assessments (I now see a maximum of four). I was designing and delivering new

$\rightarrow$

programmes for a number of corporate clients and had started writing careers articles for the national press as well as doing a few stints on radio and TV. Work was going great but my satisfaction was waning. There were no further career progression opportunities for me in the company and my close work buddies had moved on. I was also feeling a bit worn out, and most importantly, I wanted to move back to Dublin.

Cue the next dip – the move back was great for me personally but pretty challenging professionally. I started working for myself immediately but found that I really missed the support and structure of working for a company. I was also working from home and found this experience both isolated and lonely. Looking back, I can see now that I lost my professional confidence whilst I adjusted to a new way of working. I started working as a freelance consultant and I took on some projects outside of my usual remit. Not all of them suited me that well, but crucially they provided satisfaction by getting me back into a structured network, working with great people, and out of the house.

Confidence back in place, I started collaborating with my now business partner and, having enticed my old CPL colleague to join us (she was now working for a large corporate in Dublin), we now run a successful Careers Consultancy called Pinpoint. This is the up and down squiggle you see on the chart. Pinpoint has been a rollercoaster of job satisfaction and I think anyone running their own business will tell a similar story. The highs are incredible: making a breakthrough with a difficult client; getting our first 'big' job; winning jobs when competing with bigger names; working with colleagues who are also friends that you admire and trust; being able to stay true to your values and having an office in Georgian Dublin beside the canal – that all feels great.

The lows are pretty spectacular too – losing out to bigger competitors yet again when you believe you had a better offering; worrying about your diary being too full or not full enough; not getting paid on time; worrying about cash flow; a project over-running; doing a job just for the money; managing differences in opinion with colleagues who are friends you admire and trust.

But overall, it works.

Most importantly, what have I learned from it all?

- I can do a lot of jobs quite well but only a handful excellently.
- My work relationships determine my overall level of job satisfaction.
- I thrive working with good people and wilt when working alone.
- I like to be my own boss but I don't like managing others.
- I am a very good Number Two – deputy boss that is.
- I'm not terribly organised but I rarely miss a deadline.
- I am very practical and I like routine.
- I am attracted to small companies that are values-driven rather than commercially driven.
- I am not a corporate person, I don't do 'politics'.
- I operate on a seven-year cycle.

Pretty simple stuff really, but being aware of these things is very important for monitoring my current situation, and crucially for thinking ahead about what I want to invest and get out of the next seven years of my career.

That's my story – what's yours? Map *your* career highs and lows on the chart below, then ask yourself the questions on the opposite page.

What triggered a specific career high or low?

Thinking about these questions and the answers they generate is amazingly effective. Learning from your past experience about what makes you happy can work wonders for your future work happiness. When was the last time you got to think solely about your job satisfaction? Probably the last time you changed jobs, if you're like the rest of us. And how long ago was that? Very few people do this routinely. So put aside an hour or two to think about your career path to date and to document your career highs and lows. It's well worth it. Remember, this exercise is concerned only with your level of career satisfaction, not to be confused with your career progression. For some people, the two go hand in hand. But for others, career progression and career satisfaction are not necessarily linked.

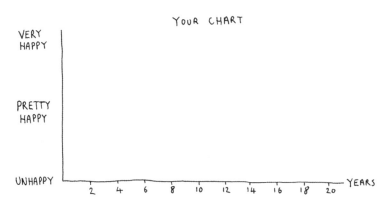

ASK YOURSELF...
What Does My Career Satisfaction Chart Tell Me?

What happened at each key stage – is there a common timeframe between each move in your chart?

What triggered a specific career high or low? Was it a job change? A promotion? Working with a new team? Learning a new skill? Going back to college? Working for a new boss?

How did you react to being very happy?

How did you react to being very unhappy?

What would you do differently this time? (This is in relation to the career lows in particular.)

What story does this chart tell? Are there more highs than lows? Why? Why not?

What have you learned about yourself from this exercise?

What would you like the remainder of your chart to look like?

Finding your internal career compass

It's easy to lose your way in your career and end up feeling a bit at sea. I've lost count of the number of times I hear clients say things like:

'I started out in the right career but somewhere along the line, it all went wrong'

'I can't even remember why I went into this career'

WHAT TRIGGERED A SPECIFIC CAREER HIGH OR LOW?

'I've never felt like I fit in at work' *or*
'I don't even know how I ended up in this job'

Think carefully about the questions on page 26. By spending some time on your self-awareness, you simply get to know yourself better, and set the scene for increasing your happiness considerably. You will get to think about where you are now compared to where you want to be. Increasing your self-awareness ensures that you hold yourself responsible for your situation and means that you are more likely to deal effectively with any career issues.

Maybe this exercise will simply remind you of some of the things that you had hoped for when you started your working life, but these have gone by the wayside over time. Like a client who, ten years into her career as an Administrator for an engineering firm, moved to the same job in a hospital and found this much more fulfilling and enjoyable. By answering the questions below, she remembered that she had always wanted to work in a caring environment. But she had taken the first job she was offered and after ten years, she was still there.

Answering the following questions will help you find your internal career compass – that intuitive sense of where you fit in the world of work, and more importantly *where you want to go*. It's your instinctive sense of career direction that sometimes gets lost amidst the business and stress of your day-to-day work. Maybe you do all of the above naturally without having to think about it. If so, good on you and keep it up! If not, the following ten questions will help you gain some important insights into where your career compass is pointing.

Be as honest and as detailed as you can in your answers. Some of the solutions will be more than obvious. Some questions may demand a little more reflection. There is no magic wand solution to being happy at work. It takes a lot of effort to keep on top of what's important to you, to be the person you want to be, and not to get sidetracked by the hustle and bustle of life.

ASK YOURSELF...
Where Is My Internal Career Compass Pointing?

Why did you choose your current career?
What were your hopes and ambitions for your career when you started work?
Who/what were the key influencers in your decision to pursue this career?
What do you want your career to offer you?
Write a list of the things you *most* enjoy about your career.
Write a list of the things you *least* enjoy about your career.
What kind of people do you most enjoy working with?
What kind of people do you least enjoy working with?
Who/what were the key influencers in your decision to take the job?
Think of a happy work situation and identify what exactly made you happy.
Think of an unhappy work situation and identify what exactly made you unhappy.

If you can't answer all of these questions comprehensively, that's fine. I hope that by the time you finish this book, you will be able to. For now, what I want you to achieve from this exercise is a heightened sense of self-awareness that will allow you to assess your current situation and reflect on the things that are going well for you and the things that aren't going so well. Throughout the Steps that follow, we will be looking at ways in which you can capitalise on what's going well and address what's not. And all of this is the starting point for a happier YOU.

What motivates you?

In order to enjoy work more, you need to identify which parts of your work make you happy. These parts of work are your *key motives*. You've already got off to a good start in identifying what makes work enjoyable for you by completing your Career Satisfaction Chart together with asking yourself where your Internal Career Compass' is pointing. So read on to find out a bit more about your work motives and how knowing what makes you tick makes you happier.

We are all driven by different things. Some of us go to work so that we can be with other people and enjoy the social and relationship side of work. Others are motivated by money or career progression, reaching the top of the pile and achieving a high-profile position in their company. Then, there are those who enjoy work because it allows them to be creative, analytical or caring. Being clear about your work motives allows you to pursue jobs, projects or opportunities that you will find energising and fulfilling, and most importantly enjoyable.

This might seems perfectly obvious, but it's amazing how often we get the simple things wrong.

WE ARE ALL DRIVEN BY DIFFERENT THINGS

Find your key work motives

So, what about *your* work motives?

To help you identify what drives your job satisfaction, I have listed a range of key work motives opposite. These exist in most work environments to a greater or lesser extent. Read through the chart and identify which ones in particular are important to you. It's also important to look at where your motives are being met, and where they're not. In the right-hand column I have listed typical work scenarios relating to each of the key motives.

Read through the chart and answer the questions as you go along. Think about the questions that 'click' with you in particular. Pick out your top five motives. Then think about your own situation and see if these are being met at work.

I have separated the Motivation Chart into three sections that relate to the three key themes of this book. This will make it easy for you to see where your key motives lie and where they are being met.

1 **Managing Yourself** → You and Your Job

2 **Managing Others** → You and Others

3 **Managing Your**
  World of Work → You and Your Organisation

Spending time answering these questions is a good investment in your work happiness and will help to identify what motivates you. If you discover that your motives aren't being met, don't panic. The steps that follow will tell you how to deal with these situations.

Work Motivation Chart

Key work motives YOU AND YOUR JOB	Find out what motivates you at work. Ask yourself the following questions...
Meaningful work	Do you find your work fulfilling?
	What percentage of your work do you enjoy?
	Are you proud of what you do?
	Does your work add something positive to your life?
Clarity of role	Are you clear about what's expected of you at work?
	Do you know how your role fits in with the aims and objectives of your team/your department/your organisation?
	Is there a clear reporting structure?
	Do you have a job description/a person specification/an organisational chart?
Realistic workload	What percentage of your work do you enjoy?
	Do you have enough work to fill your day?
	Can you complete your work in your contracted hours? Is your overtime rewarded or recognised?
Feelings of choice and control over your work	Is work allocated based on people's preferences and strengths?
	Can you opt out of projects/working groups/committees that are not benefiting from your input?
	Are there set ways in which you must do your work – Standard Operating Procedures? Can you have any input into these?
	Can you decide how and when you complete your work?
	Is there a facility for you to make suggestions about work procedures and processes?

$\rightarrow$

Key work motives YOU AND OTHERS	Find out what motivates you at work. Ask yourself the following questions...
Thanks for a job well done	Do you receive regular feedback from your boss? Do you have annual/bi-annual performance appraisals? Do you have regular review meetings or de-briefs with your colleagues after each project?
Availability of social support in the workplace	Are you friends with any of your colleagues? Do you socialise with colleagues outside of work? Is there a social club at work? Would you be willing to organise a social event outside of work? Do you and your colleagues discuss non-related work issues?
Altruistic environment/ opportunities	Is there a collaborative and supportive culture? Is there an appreciation of the non-commercial aspect of your work?
Key work motives YOU AND YOUR ORGANISATION	Find out what motivates you at work. Ask yourself the following questions...
Money	Are you being paid fairly/competitively (in line with your colleagues and the marketplace)? Do you have an annual/bi-annual salary review? Is there a bonus/share scheme/performance-related pay system in place?

Belief in your organisation	Do you know your company's mission statement?
	Are you proud to work for your company?
	Think about which of the following work environments appeal to you. Which do you feel most suits you personality and your workstyle?
	Private sector Public sector Co-operative
	Voluntary/ Large corporate Self-employed charity sector Small start-up Family business
Opportunity for career progression	Are there clear career progression paths in your organisation?
	Does your organisation invest in training and development?
	Is there a strong learning culture?

Deirdre, an accountant in her mid-thirties, provides a good example of how to use self-awareness effectively. She spent a lot of time reflecting on her work motives and gearing herself up for a career change. In the end, however, a career change wasn't the answer. Deirdre took some time in finding the right solution but the result was well worth the wait.

Deirdre's Story: Right Job – Wrong Industry

Deirdre – roving Financial Controller for GOAL, an international aid organisation with programmes running in countries across the world.

Deirdre qualified as a Chartered Accountant straight from university without putting too much thought into any other

$\rightarrow$

career path. Her family background was Law and Accountancy so one of these careers seemed like a good idea, as they both offered solid career opportunities, which was something her dad was keen for her to pursue. Having worked as an accountant in the advertising industry in Australia on her year out, on her return to Ireland, she took a job in Banking and Finance, despite her reservations about her 'fit' for the corporate world. Her instinct proved right and Deirdre spent two rather unsatisfying years at the bank thinking about what to do next.

Her next move provided her with much more satisfaction: Financial Controller for a high-end car dealership. Deirdre had always got on well with her bosses and this environment proved no exception. She soon became the General Manager's right-hand woman and after two years was promoted to Deputy GM with a view to taking over from her boss when he retired five years hence. The Deputy GM role allowed her to move outside a pure finance remit and this was both challenging and fulfilling for her. However, there was also a niggling doubt gnawing at her – as she moved closer to the top position she asked herself: 'Is this what I really want?' She was aware that she no longer got as much satisfaction from dealing with the very demanding customers as she had in the past. She also found that a lot of staff conflict issues were escalated to her, which she found emotionally very draining.

What made her unease all the more difficult was that everybody thought she had the perfect job. What with the new top-of-the-range car as part of the package – the golf trips, the fancy dinners and all the other junkets that go with working in that industry – she was the envy of most of her peers. Coupled with this, she also felt a huge debt of loyalty to her boss – after all, he had taken her under his wing and presented her with this fantastic opportunity to manage one of the most prestigious dealerships in the country. So she stayed on, not wanting to leave her boss in the lurch and not willing to leave a job before she had found a suitable alternative.

But she kept on coming back to the realisation that her heart just wasn't in it. With her accountancy qualification and her management experience, she knew there were lots of options open to her. She found herself reading lots of 'change your life and career' articles and considering a more radical career change. Should she start her own business, travel, move into retail management, go back to college, study languages (German and French had been her top subjects at school)? Despite researching all these options in depth, none of them grabbed her sufficiently for her to take the plunge. Conscious of her cautious nature, she found herself becoming more and more anxious about leaving her safe haven without something solid to move on to.

Deirdre's 'eureka' moment came one evening as she watched TV and saw a documentary on Africa which featured an international aid organisation – and focussed on the job the accountant was doing – and there was her answer. 'I was so immersed in the thought of changing career, that I didn't consider the same career in a different field. Here was something I had always thought of doing but had completely forgotten about because of the focus on change.'

$\rightarrow$

Furthermore she had a very useful set of skills to offer. The very next day, she rang around a number of aid agencies and organised interviews. Once she had arrived at the right decision, there was no procrastination, no stress, and no doubt that this was the right move for her. Four weeks later, she jetted off to Darfur to begin her first overseas assignment and hasn't looked back since. She is now a roving Financial Controller, travelling around the world to different disaster zones, managing the money side of international aid programmes. She has successfully tapped into her strong altruistic motivation whilst using her professional experience and qualifications. And as many of her assignments are based in Africa, she also gets to use her French!

What would Deirdre do differently if she had her time again?

- Bide your time before you leave an unhappy job – avoid the temptation to take the first thing that comes your way. If she had done that, she might have missed out on finding her true vocation. When the time is right, you will find that the answer is much nearer than you think. She says: 'Making the decision to join GOAL was very easy, I kept looking for reasons not to move and couldn't find any!'

- Deirdre realised that she confused loyalty and commitment with ambition. She says 'A lot of the time, it was me putting myself under pressure, not others. I now believe that no one will thank you for staying at a job out of loyalty. At the end of the day, you will be replaced and the work will go on.'

■ Follow your instinct and remember *you're* the person who has to do your job. 'I was far too caught up with what others thought of my job, which made my decision to leave a whole lot more difficult.'

This is a great example of how increased self-awareness can really improve your work life. Is there anything that you have learned from Deirdre's story that you can apply to your own situation?

That brings us to the end of Step 1. Well done! You've already covered a lot of ground. By exploring your level of self-awareness, particularly in relation to your work happiness, you have provided a solid foundation for Steps 2 to 10. You may well find yourself referring back to Step 1 and reminding yourself what you took from the Self-awareness piece, Career Satisfaction and Motivation Charts. For now though, let's move on to Step 2.

"

Most folks are about as happy as they make up their minds to be.

Abraham Lincoln

"

Choose to be Happy

02

So, how do you use the knowledge you have gained in Step 1 to make your work life more enjoyable? By being proactive. In Step 2, I'm asking you to *choose* to be happy. And once you make that choice, I want you to actively pursue it. That's really what proactivity is about and this step tells you exactly how to do this by:

■ Taking responsibility for your happiness

■ Identifying the things that make you unhappy

■ Seeing where you can use your influence to improve your situation.

Learn from missed opportunities

Have you ever looked back at a work situation and thought, 'I should have done x, y, z. . .' or 'Why didn't I?' Yes? Well, we've all been there. And what was it that you typically should have done? Probably one of the following, if my clients' experiences are anything to go by:

■ Grabbed an opportunity before it disappeared

■ Made a bold move early on in your career

■ Tackled an issue before it became a problem

■ Communicated something difficult or sensitive to a colleague or boss

■ Made an important decision instead of allowing someone else to decide for you

■ Trusted your instinct and acted upon it

■ Fixed a relationship

■ Taken a chance or a risk

■ Had the confidence to say 'Yes' or 'No'

... the list goes on.

What all of these scenarios have in common is that at a critical point, you possibly did or said nothing. And often this leaves you with a sense of a missed opportunity. And this is where proactivity comes in.

Be proactive

In his excellent book, *The 7 Habits of Highly Effective People*, Stephen Covey stresses the importance of proactivity in dealing with any work situation. Being proactive means taking responsibility for yourself, focusing on your situation, and clearly identifying what you want to achieve. This is the starting point. Planning how you will achieve your desired outcome (more of which in Step 3) and then doing it is the natural follow-on. That makes sense doesn't it? Proactivity maximises your chance of getting what you want out of work.

PROACTIVITY MAXIMISES YOUR CHANCE OF GETTING WHAT YOU WANT OUT OF WORK

Being proactive enhances your career satisfaction

A proactive approach to career satisfaction means identifying what makes you happy (using Step 1 as a starting point) and then working out what is getting in the way of that happiness (using the Tackling your Concerns exercise below). In short, you're going to examine your situation fully and use your new-found knowledge to remove the unhappiness factors and add in more happiness ones.

What makes you unhappy?

So what are your unhappiness factors? These are the parts of your job that you can't stand. Do any of the following seem at all familiar?

- the unreasonable boss
- the lack of opportunities for creativity in your role
- the irritating colleague
- the lack of career progression
- the salary you earn
- the hours you work
- the commute

the list goes on ...

Some or all of these together can add up to real unhappiness in your career, but there is something you can do to address them.

Tackling your concerns

I want you to think about what makes you unhappy at work. Covey calls these your 'Concerns'. List them on a sheet of paper and draw a circle around them. We'll call this your Circle of Concern. The idea here is that you identify what goes into the Circle of Concern and then decide what can be done about it. It might seem simpler to accept these concerns as a given within your situation and either ignore them or try to work around them, but that seriously reduces your chances of being happy. So, roll up your sleeves, it's time to take the bull by the horns!

As you draw up your list, try to separate it into two sections: (a) things you can change and (b) things you think you can't. The aim of this exercise is to try and take as many concerns as possible from your Circle of Concern and move them into your Sphere of Influence. Your Sphere of Influence houses the gripes on your list that you can improve in some way.

In order to move an item from your Circle of Concern to your Sphere of Influence, you need to find a solution to resolve your concern and commit to following through with action. For example, a concern might be that your salary is too low. Moving this concern to your Sphere of Influence means finding a way to increase your earning power. Your initial reaction might be that there's nothing you can do about it, but is that really the case? Is there a way for you to earn more money? What solutions can you come up with to increase your earning potential? (See Your Proactivity Chart below for some ideas.)

Your Proactivity Chart

Okay, it's time for action. Let's use your list of concerns as a starting point and see how to move them into your Sphere of Influence. The chart overleaf lists a number of common concerns; things we all face at work from time to time. Working through the chart from left to right, it shows the consequences of being proactive versus being reactive or doing nothing. I've provided a number of solutions to each concern to get you started. Now, I want you to go though the list and ask yourself: do these solutions work for me? Thinking about your own situation, see what solutions you can add.

Can you find a way to improve your work life by addressing your concerns?

The Proactivity Chart has been divided into three sections that relate to the three key themes of this book, making it easier for you to see where your key concerns are.

1 **Managing Yourself**   →   You and Your Job

2 **Managing Others**   →   You and Others

3 **Managing Your**   →   You and Your World of Work
  World of Work

Maybe some of the concerns listed above apply to your situation; maybe there are other things that concern you. The important thing is to be crystal clear about what makes you unhappy (your concerns) and to work out what can be done about them (being proactive and using your influence). Sometimes the conclusion will be that changing a situation is beyond your control. That's fine, you'll find that it's easier to put up with it if you know you can't change it. It's when you ignore a concern that could easily be tackled that you may feel frustrated. So the important thing is that you get into the habit of assessing where and when you can use your influence to create a happier work life for you.

In a nutshell a proactive approach to your work means that you acknowledge and appreciate what makes you happy and face up to what makes you unhappy. Choosing to use your influence to fix things that make you unhappy empowers you and is key to your happiness. Being proactive is a natural follow-on from self-awareness. Once you have the right self-knowledge about what works well for you and what doesn't, you can use it to make your work life happier.

GET INTO THE HABIT OF ASSESSING WHERE AND WHEN YOU CAN USE YOUR INFLUENCE TO CREATE A HAPPIER WORK LIFE

Your Proactivity Chart

Concerns – the things that get in the way of your work happiness	
1. YOU and YOUR JOB	**Be proactive – use your influence**
The part of your job that you can't stand	If you work as part of a team – can you allocate tasks by preference?
	Specialise/become expert in your preferred task a■ so you are more likely to be assigned your preferr■ task.
	Informally swap tasks within a team if appropriate
Poor confidence in your ability to do your job well	Is your lack of confidence based on a real or perceived inability to do your job well?
	Seek constructive feedback from your colleagues and your boss.
	Identify the strongest person on your team and buddy up with them on tasks that need improvement.
	Use the training and development or coaching resources in your company to up-skill.
	Address the issue constructively with your boss.
	Think about whether or not you're suited to the r■ – are you a square peg in a round hole?

nsequence of action	Reactive solution – do nothing	Consequence of no action
u spend less time ing the parts of your) you dislike.	Do nothing.	Your job stays the same until your boss/company decides to change it.
parate confidence ue from competence you may find you're t as good at your) as everyone else. /our performance eds some provement, you take nstructive action to nedy this through ining and velopment, entoring, work-adowing.	Do nothing.	Your job stays the same until your boss/company decides to change it. Confidence decreases with time.

$\rightarrow$

2. YOU and OTHERS	
Feeling overlooked/ neglected	You need to get noticed, and to do that you need to talk and communicate with people more.
	Organise weekly updates with your team and/or boss to discuss progress where you can highlight your input to tasks and projects. You can also do this by email if you work remotely/off-site.
	Ask for feedback from colleagues and boss regularly.
	Suggest quarterly presentations to other teams or departments.
	Get involved with your colleagues on a social level
The unreasonable boss	You don't have to like your boss – but you can work on your professional relationship.
	Seek to find common ground – do you share any interests outside of work that you can 'bond' over
	Explain clearly to your boss, using specific example why you feel the demands being made are unreasonable.
The colleague who drives you mad	Are your irritations about this person reasonable? Reflect on your behaviour towards this person.
	Accept people's differences.
	Try to improve your relationship with colleagues – find common ground.

ilds better mmunication annels between you d your boss and lleagues. ovides a vehicle for eaningful feedback m boss and lleagues. ilds better ationships with lleagues and boss.	Do nothing.	Become more invisible at work. Feel more isolated as time goes on.
proves your ationship with your ss – keeps your cus on being ofessional about ationships at work.	Do nothing.	Maybe your boss fixes the relationship *or* Your relationship with your boss stays the same at best but maybe deteriorates over time.
proves your ationship with your lleagues – keeps ur focus on being ofessional about ationships at work.	Do nothing.	Maybe your colleague fixes the relationship or changes for the better or your relationship with your colleague stays the same at best or maybe deteriorates with time.

$\rightarrow$

3. YOU and YOUR WORLD OF WORK

Lack of jobs/career prospects in your industry	Identify your transferable skills set. Diversify within your own company. Retrain in order to change career.
Lack of career progression	Go for all available promotions inside and outside your organisation. Up-skill through in-house training and development. Undertake further professional or academic qualifications. Get yourself a mentor or a coach.
The company mission statement, with which you fundamentally disagree	Progress to a senior level and seek to change it from within. Use the employee suggestion box to review mission statement. Move to an organisation whose values are more in line with your own.
The salary you earn	Seek an annual salary review. Keep up to date with what the market pays and communicate this to your boss/HR. Do overtime. Take on nixers/freelance work if your contract allows it. Seek a better-paying job – find out who's the top remunerator in your industry.

oens up the ossibility of a career version/career ange for you.	Do nothing.	You get head-hunted. You stay in the same job – maybe get stuck in a rut – it becomes harder to change or tackle the situation as time goes on.
proves your career ospects in your own mpany. hances the offer you ve to make to nployers in general.	Do nothing.	Job stays the same – career opportunities and prospects fade with time.
eates the potential influence change er time.	Accept it – not much you can do about this one. Hard to influence what goes on at a corporate level unless you operate at that level yourself.	Accept it. Focus on the parts of your job/organisation that make up for this mismatch with the values of your organisation. If not, you need to think about a move.
ows you to increase ur earnings potential.	Do nothing.	Earn the same salary whilst the cost of living/inflation rises.

$\rightarrow$

3. YOU and YOUR WORLD OF WORK (Continued)

The hours you work	Stick to your contracted hours.
	Do not subscribe to the overwork culture if it exists in your company.
	Explore flexible working.
	Flag extra hours worked to your boss if it's an ongoing situation.
	Where appropriate, seek some reward and recognition for extra hours worked.
The commute to work	Is your job flexible – can you work from home one or two days a week?
	Car pool to reduce driving and save on cost.
	Take public transport and read a book on the way and from work. Less stressful on your system.
	Move nearer to work!
List your own concerns here	**Be proactive – use your influence**

Please note that all of these concerns will be dealt with in more depth throughout the Steps that follow.

ows you to actively onitor your input and oid falling into the bit of overwork.	Again, hard to influence this part of your work life, particularly if your contract dictates set hours.	You end up working more than your contracted hours – possibly for no extra reward or recognition. Overwork leads to stress and exhaustion over time.
u spend less time mmuting plus you plore the potential doing some work m home.	Do nothing.	Time spent in heavy traffic is unproductive and stressful.
nsequence of action	Reactive solution – do nothing	Consequence of no action

What can you change?

What you can realistically change will vary. Influencing your company mission statement or the hours you work is a much bigger task than dealing with an irritating colleague. In general, you can influence your immediate situation (your job and those around you) more easily. See if the solutions outlined above are appropriate for your situation. If not, can you think what might be? Deciding where you can use your influence is a useful exercise in itself but obviously putting your influence into action is the real goal. (We'll discuss this in more depth in Step 3 – Habits and Goal-Setting). It takes courage and discipline to tackle your concerns, so taking on any more than three at a time may prove difficult. On the plus side, using your influence in one situation will often have a positive knock-on effect on other parts of your work life. John's story provides a good example of this.

John came to me for career coaching. Look at how he tackled a problematic work situation and the positive outcome he achieved. Is there a similar situation in your work life that could do with the same approach?

IT WILL TAKE COURAGE AND DISCIPLINE TO TACKLE YOUR CONCERNS

John's Story: Proactive versus Reactive?

John had taken on a new job as assistant in a busy accounts department. He enjoyed his job greatly, was good at it and got on well with his colleagues. One of his tasks was to reconcile the petty cash on a weekly basis. This involved collecting receipts from all the accounts team and totting up the petty cash bills. He soon noticed that one of his team members took great pleasure in belittling him when he did this task by saying things like 'Don't forget your 12 times tables' or 'See if you can do it without a calculator this week' or 'Everyone keep quiet now, John's doing his homework'.

After a few weeks, he began to dread the weekly task but, being reserved by nature and new in the role, he let the comments go on, week after week. By the time he came to see me six months later, he was considering jacking in his job. Even though this was the only blip in an otherwise fulfilling and satisfying job, the negative significance attached to this one task had left him feeling that he had little option but to quit.

We discussed what other options might be available, the obvious one being to tackle the situation head on. He said there was no point. He argued that he was still relatively new in the role, he was shy and less senior than his tormentor, who was really popular in the team. He had already told the boss about it (and she had advised him to ignore it). His options as he saw then were to put up with it or leave. After some persuasion, he agreed to work with me on this. We spent one session (an hour) working on how he could take

$\rightarrow$

control of the situation and then preparing and practising what to say and how to say it.

The following Friday afternoon, at the allotted time, he collected the receipts. When he came to his tormentor, she started her usual banter. He let her finish, and said 'Polly, I do this task every week, it's an important part of my job and I do it well. From now on I'd like you to stop passing comments as it makes me feel uncomfortable'. Polly's snide comments stopped from that day on and John was left to get back to enjoying his job.

I like John's example because it really demonstrates how exerting your influence over small situations can have far-reaching consequences. Here was someone who used his influence by simply saying 'Stop'. And in doing so, he prevented himself the significant upheaval and anxiety that changing jobs entails. In using his influence in this very straightforward manner, John was able not just to address a concern, but to remove that concern completely from his work life. He described this as being a very empowering experience and one that gave him the confidence to address other concerns on an ongoing basis.

Can you say 'Stop'?

Think about your own work situation. Does John's story inspire you to speak out? Being proactive and using your influence *is* empowering and builds confidence. Is there a situation that's bothering you that you can tackle in a straightforward way? As in John's story, sometimes simply asking a colleague to stop (or start, or continue for that matter) a certain behaviour is all it takes to improve a situation.

Being proactive is good for your career too ...

As well as making you happier, being proactive will also help you to get ahead in your career. People who are proactive are more likely to monitor and evaluate their career progression. If you've been in the same organisation or career for a long time, you often take your skills and experience for granted. And remember, if you undervalue yourself and what you have to offer, others will too.

Update your profile

One thing I advise my clients to do on an annual basis is to create or add to their professional profile on an annual basis. Highlight and write down your key successes and contributions over the past 12 months. Be sure to highlight tangible outcomes or results. For example, instead of 'looked after staff payroll' you could say something like 'managed the monthly payroll system for 400 people companywide including the resolution of any pay queries within one week'. I'm sure you'll be pleasantly surprised at just how industrious you have been.

Do this as if you were going for a new job, so that you will present and promote your skills appropriately. This will keep your career strengths and achievements to the fore and fill you with a sense of confidence. This will benefit you greatly when you are faced with a challenging situation at work, such as taking on a new project or going for an internal promotion. What you will inevitably find is that a proactive approach is a sure-fire way of energising your career efforts and creating a happier you at work.

Being proactive about your work happiness is probably one of the best career decisions you will ever make. Deciding to fix, improve or change a situation is more empowering than you possibly realise. Try it and see what happens.

Deciding to be happy and actively pursuing it sets you up nicely for Step 3, which is all about *doing.* That means making new happiness habits that will stick and goal-setting in your quest for a happier you.

Onwards and upwards; Step 3 beckons…

A PROACTIVE APPROACH IS A SURE-FIRE WAY OF ENERGISING YOUR CAREER EFFORTS

You are what you repeatedly do.

Aristotle

Your Happiness Plan

03

We'll finish Section 1, Managing Yourself, by consolidating the learning from Steps 1 and 2 (Self-awareness and Proactivity). We'll do this by looking at ways in which to turn a commitment to change into an action for change. The previous steps have provided you with a solid foundation for positive change, which is now firmly within your grasp. In short, the focus is firmly on *doing*.

In this Step, you will find the confidence and ability to plan and practise your own set of happiness habits. How do you do that? By setting some goals (using a success-guaranteed method called SMART). You'll also look at how to introduce some really useful happiness habits into your work life. And you'll conclude Step 3, the last step in Section 1 – Managing Yourself – by making these new habits a permanent fixture in your life. That includes some great techniques about proactively managing yourself and your work happiness.

Goal-setting

Did you know that your job satisfaction soars when you are achieving the goals you set yourself? In time and with practice, we want goal-setting to become a core part of the new proactive you. In Step 2, you looked at your situation and identified the obstacles to your happiness (we've called these your 'Concerns'). And you've seen that it's possible to remove them by using your influence over the situation. By removing the obstacles to your work satisfaction, you are firmly on the road to building a happier work future for yourself. Now that you've subtracted the concerns, let's look at how you can *add* to the parts of work that you enjoy, which brings us on to the subject of goal setting.

So, what is it that will make you happier at work? Think about the things that would add to your experience of work. For any good plan to succeed, the critical first step is clarifying your goal. Don't automatically assume that your goal has to be about climbing the career ladder, earning more money or being more 'successful' (although these are all valid goals too). It might just as easily be about getting on better with your team or your boss, working on a particular project, or getting that further qualification under your belt at long last.

What's your career wish-list?

A good starting point to help you identify your goal or goals is to create a career wish-list. This should help you to clearly visualise and define what you want to achieve. In career terms, short-term goals are anything you want to achieve in the next 6 to 12 months; medium-term goals are 1–3 years and long-term goals are 3-7 years. Set yourself goals that are challenging enough to engage you fully but also realistic and achievable with the resources and time available to you. Your goals should also be in line with your work motives so there is a natural drive to achieve them.

THE CRITICAL FIRST STEP IS CLARIFYING YOUR GOAL

Break it down

Break your goals down into smaller steps to make them more manageable and time bound. Think about and plan for any obstacles. And highlight the support, resources and people that you can depend on in order to guarantee your success. Lastly, review your progress at regular intervals to make sure you're on track – three-monthly checks are a good idea.

Focus on outcomes

It's always a good idea to check your goals by asking yourself, 'What do I want this goal to enable me to do?' So instead of making your goal 'Learning how to use Excel', make it about *why* you want to learn this. So your goal becomes 'I want to produce Excel spreadsheet reports for the sales team for the annual report which is due to be presented at the AGM in four months' time'. What you're focusing on is the *outcome* of the goal, and what your goal will allow you to do.

SMART goals for a happier you

Let's look at SMART goal-setting, which is a sure-fire way of setting outcome-driven goals.

- Identify and write down your goal. What is the outcome you want to achieve from this goal?
- Does your goal fit the SMART criteria? SMART is …

- **Specific** – can you pinpoint the outcome you want to achieve?
- **Measurable** – can you measure this outcome objectively? What are the key milestones you need to hit?
- **Achievable** – is it a realistic goal, given your skills and resources?
- **Results-oriented** – what is the key function of your goal?
- **Time-bound** – do you have a timeframe or deadline allocated to the goal?

Let's look at the example above and put it into the SMART framework to see how it works.

Your goal is 'to produce Excel spreadsheet reports for the sales team for the annual report which is due to be presented at the AGM in four months' time' (see next page).

How to make SMART work for you

I think you'll agree that using the SMART framework really motivates you towards making changes to your work life that *will* make you happier. You'll find that the step-by-step approach makes your goal more achievable by pinpointing the critical points you need to hit on the way to achieving your goal. It's also useful to identify the support available to you and to trouble-shoot any potential problems before you get going on your goals. You'll be pleased to know that SMART goal-setting is made easier by the work you have already done on Concerns and Proactivity.

SMART goal-setting

Write down your goal	'I want to produce spreadsheet reports for the sales team for the annual report which is due to be presented at the AGM in four months' time.'
Is your goal SMART?	**Specific** – Yes, to produce spreadsheet reports **Measurable** – Yes, publication of these reports in the annual report. **Achievable** – Yes, if I can do a course in Excel and get support from the in-house IT trainers plus my own team and manager. **Results–oriented** – Yes, reports will supply important information for sales team. **Time-bound** – Yes, the AGM is in four months' time.
What are the key milestones to achieving your goal?	Learn to use Excel. Learn to produce sales reports. Get sign-off from my manager. Submit to the marketing department for publication in the annual report.
Identify support/resources available to you to achieve your goal	Training course in Excel. Ongoing technical support from my team, manager and in-house IT trainers. Use the internet and software support for trouble-shooting technical problems.

Identify any potential obstacles to achieving your goal	Not able to go on the course if too busy at work.
	Colleagues/IT trainers too busy to help me.
Re-visit, review and refine your goal (in light of resources available and obstacles present)	OK to stick to original goal.
Track your progress – carry out a three-monthly review	Went on course and on track. Have draft reports ready for sign-off from manager.
Measure your outcome against your initial goal	Got sign-off from manager who suggested some minor changes. Implemented changes with the support of colleague.
Measure your outcome against your revised goal	Submitted reports to marketing department and included in annual report.

In a way, it's the final piece of the jigsaw as you move from one stage of self-awareness to the next. Look at the natural sequence of events so far:

- Reflect on your situation
- Decide what will make you happier
- Identify what's standing in the way of your happiness
- Set goals to become happier
- Put those goals into action.

ASK YOURSELF...
How Can I Achieve My SMART Goals?

What are the key milestones to achieving your goal?

What are the support and resources available to you to enable you to achieve your goal?

What are the potential obstacles to your achieving your goal?

What is your timeframe? Do you need to have a contingency timeframe?

Throughout the timeframe, do the following ...

■ Re-visit, review and refine your goal (in light of resources available and obstacles present).

■ Track your progress – carry out a three-monthly review.

■ Measure your outcome against your initial goal.

■ Measure your outcome against your revised goal.

The SMART approach gives you a fail-safe framework for:

■ Addressing your concerns

■ Identifying what will make you happier

■ Being proactive about achieving your goals.

Thinking about your own situation, answer the following three questions:

1 What would make me happier at work?

2 What is the goal that will support this?

3 What outcome do I want to achieve?

Use SMART to help you define and plan your goals. I generally advise clients to aim to work on one short-term and one long-term goal every 18 months. You will find that working towards goals improves your job satisfaction significantly.

Even taking small steps, as long as they are in the right direction, will get you to your destination.

Remember, the man who moved a mountain started by carrying away pebbles.

Create new happiness habits

As well as setting regular goals for yourself, another great way to make sure that your work life is as pleasant as possible is to learn some quick-fix happiness habits. These are little things that make a big difference to your working day. You will find that you can easily make these a part of your everyday routine.

21 days is all it takes

Did you know that it takes 21 days to form a new habit? That's not a long time to invest in a life- or work-enhancing initiative, is it? Habits are defined as frequent repetition of behaviours that become automatic routines in everyday life. In terms of building a happier work life, can you form new habits easily? The answer is a resounding yes! First, of course, you need to be motivated to change. Well, we all want to be happier, so that's not hard. So, what next? Well, let's look at some practical ways to make happiness habits part of your everyday life.

Your happiness at work action plan

OK, it's time for action – let's think about some real-life happiness habits. In a recent BBC TV series, *Making Slough Happy*, the programme makers worked with six happiness experts, from a variety of disciplines from Psychology to Economics, to work towards improving the happiness levels of people in the UK town of Slough. Part of this social experiment concerned the creation of a Happiness Manifesto for everyday use. Including ten items, the rationale was that doing the majority of these things for 21 days makes you happier.

I really like this list because it can be applied to any and every work environment, and it clearly demonstrates one of *Happy at Work*'s key messages, that the smallest of actions can make a big difference.

I have taken the ten items on the manifesto and looked at possibilities for integrating them into your work-day. Are you ready to take the Happiness Manifesto challenge? Read through the list and pick out three things to try in the next 21 days.

THE SMALLEST OF ACTIONS CAN MAKE A BIG DIFFERENCE

SMILING AND LAUGHING IS A GREAT DE-STRESSOR

Get physical: exercise for half an hour three times a week	Introduce a walking club at work and take lunch-time walks.
	Join a gym near work with one of your colleagues and motivate each other to go twice a week.
	Sign up for yoga, pilates, aerobics or a spin class with one of your colleagues.
	Organise a volleyball tournament at work – great for fitness, team-building and morale boosting.
	Cycle to work – eco-friendly and saves a fortune. Or take public transport to work so that you get to walk to and from the train or bus station – and again good for the environment.
Count your blessings: at the end of each day, reflect on at least five things you're grateful for	This is very effective. No matter how bad your work situation is, challenge yourself to come up with five good things that happen to you each day. Doing this reminds you to highlight the positive and not get sucked into a purely negative frame of mind. Even small things like having a nice lunch, beating the rush-hour traffic, or catching up with an old workmate can put a positive spin on your day.
Talk time: have an hour-long uninterrupted conversation with your partner or closest friend each week	The two most important relationships for creating a happy work environment are your closest colleague and your boss. Nurture your work relationships by organising mid-week lunches or after-work activities. It's easy to chat to your best work buddy but try and ensure that you talk to your boss at least once a day.

$\rightarrow$

Plant something, even if it's a window box or pot plant. Keep it alive!	Keep a plant on your desk and look after it! If you don't have plants in the office or the common areas, suggest to your boss that your office goes green. Not only do plants improve the quality of the air you breathe, but research has shown that your physical work environment impacts significantly on your work well-being.
Cut your TV viewing by half	Cut your internet surfing by half. Workers spend on average 20 per cent of their work-day surfing the net and much of this is spent fuelling your consumer instincts via exposure to advertising and on-line shopping. Bhutan's top spot on the global Happiness Index is widely attributed to a national ban on advertising. Go figure…
Phone a friend: make contact with at least one friend or relation you have not been in contact with for a while and arrange to meet up	Has a work friend moved department, or moved company? Keep in touch every now and again by phone or by email. It's life-affirming for people to know that they haven't been forgotten about the moment they're out of your line of vision, so this works for you and for them.
	Companies that hold annual lunches for retired staff members report increased morale amongst current staff members who attend those lunches. Valuing ex-employees and recognising their contribution displays strong loyalty and commitment on the part of the company and shows current employees that their contribution will be valued after they have left the company.

Smile at and/or say hello to a stranger at least once each day	Do you look at your feet when you get into the lift? Do you ignore a fellow employee at the bus-stop because you only know them to see? Do you greet the person you buy your daily coffee/scone/newspaper from? Take the plunge and say hello. You don't even need to have a chat. It's common courtesy to acknowledge people you come across on a day-to-day basis, and heart-warming for you and the other person.
Have a good laugh at least once a day	All work and no play make Jack and Jill dull. Surround yourself with fun people. Especially if you work in a high-stress area, take some time out for some light-hearted banter – it's an important part of bonding with colleagues. Smiling and laughing is a great de-stressor and using humour cements work relationships.
	Seeing the funny side of difficult situations is also a good way to keep people engaged and motivated, instead of feeling defeated or deflated. High-stress workers such as those involved in the emergency services often use humour as a useful stress-buster.

→

Every day make sure you give yourself a treat. Take time to really enjoy this.	A cappuccino or some chocolate (or even better a herbal tea) to beat the 3pm slump, a fancy lunch with colleagues every now and then, a taxi home from work on a Friday … reward yourself with a treat every day as a reminder of your unique skills and talents.
Daily kindness: do an extra good turn for someone each day	Much of the happiness research points to the role of kindness in making you happier (see Step 5). It's no surprise to hear therefore that those involved in vocational or caring careers count themselves amongst the most contented of workers. Think about how you can practise kindness in your workplace. See if giving or sharing makes you happier by helping a colleague to meet a deadline; offering someone from the office a lift home; making an extra effort to help a new colleague settle in; or including people who are on the outskirts of a workgroup. These are all ways of making life more pleasant for the people around you – and in doing so, you benefit from the resulting feel-good factor.

Rise to the challenge and you will notice a difference within a few weeks. All you need to do is pick out three or four things that you can easily make part of your working day and practise these habits two to three times a week. Practising these habits is a good starting point for making a genuine transition to a happier you. My clients often remark how the smallest things, like starting a yoga class, doing a good turn for a colleague, or giving up TV for a few weeks, can act as a catalyst for real and lasting improvement in their general sense of well being. Try it and see for yourself!

You're coming to the end of Step 3, and this is the final step in Section 1, Managing Yourself. So it makes sense to finish this section by talking about self-management. I want to talk you through some general tips and tools that will help you keep your happiness on track.

We are all managers

First, what is management? Definitions abound but my personal favourite is simply 'the art of getting things done'. We are all managers of one sort or another, whether it's managing a team of people, your time, or your department budget. Getting things done is obviously crucial, but it's not the only function of management. In my experience, the best managers get things done *and* keep their team happy. For me, getting the job done or being successful in your role is the easy part; I would consider the happiness part of the management job more important. Why? Because in my experience, success tenaciously follows people who are fulfilled, challenged and *happy* in what they do.

Manage yourself into a happier place

Self-management is vital in creating a happy work life. But what does self-management mean? *Making a plan of action that will serve as a guide to the achievement of individual goals.* Which, if you look at what you have worked through in *Happy at Work* so far, means identifying what will make you happy and actively pursuing it. You've already done lots of work on this already, so you're well set for the last challenge of Section 1 – Managing Yourself.

After years of working with people on improving their job satisfaction, I have often been struck by the way some people naturally and effortlessly create job satisfaction for themselves, while others don't. What I've observed is that positive self-management is one of the key techniques they use. And as you know, imitation is the greatest form of flattery, so let's simply copy what they do.

Think SMILE!

SMILE Strive to Motivate, Inspire, Lead and Energise

Strive

The message here is about being proactive and not waiting for happiness to land on your desk. Actively seek out opportunities to create a happier work life for yourself.

Motivate

Consciously work on your level of motivation. Remind yourself of what motivates and drives your happiness and job satisfaction. Seek out people and situations at work that incorporate your happiness motives.

Inspire

Be an inspiration to yourself. Set yourself challenging goals and acknowledge your successes and the resulting job satisfaction. Regularly remind yourself of these successes and the happiness you felt about your achievements when you are facing the next challenge.

Lead

Instead of looking to others for leadership, pretend your boss is away and look to yourself for solutions. Get used to analysing situations you are faced with, thinking about your desired solutions and making decisions. Psychologists have found a clear link between goal-setting, decision-making and job satisfaction.

Energise

Do all of this with dynamism and energy, even if you don't feel like it. Trying to be happier can be tiring because it means using energy and proactivity. Remember though, just as success breeds success, happiness breeds happiness, so the extra effort is worth it!

REMEMBER THOUGH, JUST AS SUCCESS BREEDS SUCCESS, HAPPINESS BREEDS HAPPINESS

The SMILE mantra works in all sorts of situations, not just self-managing but also managing others – more of which in Section 2.

Congratulations, we're at the end of Section 1 – Managing Yourself. You've covered a lot of ground so far. In Step 1, the key theme was increasing your self-awareness and identifying what drives your work satisfaction. In Step 2, you took a good look at your current work situation and identified areas that could be improved and you committed to undertake these changes by using your influence. And in Step 3, you looked in depth at how to make happiness habits and goals a permanent part of your work life.

Moving on to Section 2 – Managing Others – we turn the focus from *you* to *your relationships,* and look at how to make your workplace relationships the best and happiest they can be.

MANAGING OTHERS

Section 02

STEP 4	The art of effective communication
STEP 5	Optimism and kindness: a winning combination
STEP 6	Managing your boss
STEP 7	Managing difficult relationships

Our relationships with those around us at work have a huge impact on our well-being. Think back to a time when you had some kind of conflict with a colleague – how did you feel? It's probably not something you were able to shrug off lightly and it might have left you feeling miserable and frustrated. On the other hand, think about a time when you got on really well with someone at work. Perhaps it was a time when you worked well together on a project or maybe it was just a catch-up over coffee. It will have certainly given your day a lift and made you feel positive about being at work.

Positive and effective communication at work is *the* cornerstone of happiness in the workplace. It is essential to grasp that communication is so much more than the transfer of information. It is the foundation of all our relationships; it is the vehicle we use to influence situations and other people (remember Step 2?) – and it is the lifeblood of a happy environment.

Section 2 is all about how you communicate at work and my aim is to help you build positive and productive relationships in your working world. I'll be giving you lots of tips and tools to improve your everyday interactions, as well as more in-depth help on how to understand and influence behaviours to ensure that you form strong and satisfying relationships with your colleagues – no matter what job or level.

We will look at how to communicate assertively and positively with your colleagues (Step 4); how to be optimistic in your dealings with others and practise kindness in the workplace (Step 5); how to manage your boss, using your influence and giving feedback (Step 6); and how to deal with difficult relationships (Step 7).

The art of effective communication

04

Time and time again, when I talk to people about their career satisfaction high-points, a colleague or boss's communication style will feature in the conversation. My clients often say things like:

'That was a really fun place to work, there was always a good bit of banter going on – it was 5 o'clock before you knew it.'

'I really admired my boss, she was tough but fair and although we didn't always see eye to eye, she never allowed it to become personal, and I respected her for that.'

'I was really happy on that team. Our manager always gave clear instructions and told us exactly where we were in relation to our goals. It was really important for the morale of the team as we had pretty tough deadlines to meet throughout the project.'

Sadly, these glowing accounts of communication at work are often not the case and a huge proportion of job dissatisfaction is due to neutral or negative communication centred around:

- Not knowing or not feeling included or involved in what's going on
- Not being recognised for your input or feeling listened to
- The presence of negative behaviours such as rudeness, aggression or bullying.

Every single interaction with every single person during your working day serves to either weaken or strengthen the ties between you. Fact. And your way of communicating is paramount to the success of these relationships.

The basic communication rules

Communication is a two-way process – giving and receiving messages. When you start a communication, you have full control over how your message is transmitted but not, crucially, over how it's received. That's up to the other person. And vice versa. So you are 50 per cent in control of any interaction.

That's a pretty high chance of things going wrong, so you need to make sure you are aware of some essential communication rules before starting out.

When you do the talking …
Get your fact rights

It is essential that you get names, job titles and job information correct before striking up a conversation. We all know how awkward it is to be caught out when you should know someone's name and what they do, but haven't taken the time to commit it to memory. Equally, we all know how bad it feels when we are on the receiving end of this – it makes us feel unimportant and we don't warm to the person who made this mistake.

Keep it simple

Sometimes this is easier said than done, but one of people's pet hates is waffle. We are all pressed for time and nobody likes to listen while someone laboriously works their way to a point.

When you are trying to get your point across, think about the 5 Ws: What, When, Who, Where and Why? And remember **KISS:** Keep It Short and Simple – this works for every audience.

It's not just what you say, it's how you say it …

The 'how' of the message (how the message is delivered) is just as important as the 'what' (the content of the message). It's a simple thing but easily overlooked in a work situation.

REMEMBER KISS: KEEP IT SHORT AND SIMPLE

You may be surprised to hear that the verbal message (words) accounts for only 7 per cent of the message heard by others, whilst body language and tone of voice make up a whopping 93 per cent of the emotional message (that is, the meaning picked up by the recipient). The implications of this are huge, so it's crucial you know how to use your body and voice in your day-to-day interactions.

Think how many times you have reported on an interaction by saying things like 'You should have heard how she spoke to the team' or 'John looked furious when he heard the report hadn't gone in'. It is well worth remembering that words can easily be overshadowed or the meaning lost entirely by the stronger non-verbal signals being transmitted.

Anybody in the public eye, politicians in particular, pay great attention to this aspect of their public performance as they are aware of the influencing potential of *how* a message is delivered as well as what is said. **Posture**, **tone of voice** and **eye contact** are the three critical features of non-verbal communications. Standing up straight and looking people in the eye while you are speaking to them is important, as is speaking calmly and clearly.

Stick to the facts

Too many work conversations lose their direction because the emotional content of the message takes centre-stage and distracts from the real message. This is especially true where you are making a complaint or dealing with a difficult or sensitive issue (more of which in Step 6).

Always avoid having a conversation when you are in an emotional frame of mind. Instead, step away from the situation (or the person), register your feelings and *why* you feel like that. It's a good idea to write this down to see if there is a pattern of emotion around certain tasks or people. Choose another time to address the situation and schedule a chat with your boss or colleague.

Don't get emotional

The challenge when delivering an emotional message is to provide hard and fast *evidence* as to why you felt that way. For example, instead of saying 'I can't believe you left me out of the thank-yous – you never appreciate the extra work I put in', try 'I was disappointed that my contribution to that report wasn't acknowledged at the meeting as I worked late three times last week to help the team meet the deadline.' Emotional messages hold more power when they are delivered non-emotively and backed up by specific evidence.

When you do the listening
Listen, listen and then listen some more

Sometimes the most effective way of building relationships is to say very little or nothing at all and to allow the other person to talk.

How many times have you been at a meeting where you have spent the majority of the time going through what *you* are going to say whilst completely missing out on what's actually being said by other people? Do yourself a huge favour and do your preparation and your rehearsal *before* the meeting. That way you can use your time at the meeting to observe, listen and absorb what is being said by others. This will allow you pick up on the non-verbal dynamic of the meeting and to position or tweak your message accordingly.

The best communicators do not simply deliver a pre-prepared message; they refer constantly to what's been said by others to show that they've listened and heard input from their colleagues.

Ask questions

Asking questions is key to relating to others – their answers will provide you with all sorts of useful information you can use to build the relationship. But asking questions requires much more than a cursory question mark at the end of a thought before launching into your own point of view. Make a habit of asking questions in all situations – as opposed to simply stating your ideas, opinions and feedback.

Asking is including

In your next meeting or conversation, try to ask a sincere, relevant question before putting forward your own point of view. The topic of your question might include gathering more information, clarifying a statement or perspective that someone shared, or asking for other participants' thoughts. You will notice how the tone of the meeting changes, and how people respond to being included in this process.

You will often hear bosses and managers in particular asking their team 'What do you think?' More often than not, they have their own ideas about the correct course of action, but good bosses are interested in your ideas too. This is empowering to the team member and serves to improve trust, openness and morale.

Ask, don't interrogate

Thoughtful questions are a powerful tool for learning more and fostering understanding, but no one likes to be interrogated. As with any other communication tool, be aware of your own motive for asking the question (e.g. genuinely seeking information versus trying to catch someone out), as well as the tone of your voice, body language and choice of language.

So, lots of useful tips and tools for you to use in your day-to-day interactions with colleagues. Try them out and see what happens. Once you've mastered these basic communication rules, you'll be well on your way to establishing great channels of communication at work and you'll be amazed at how much better you feel because of it.

How to behave

Along with your basic rules of communication, there are certain types of behaviour we all practise that can work for or against us when we communicate with others. To be a good communicator, you need to ensure you are using the most effective mode of behaviour to communicate.

Our behaviour can be divided into three categories: **passive, assertive and aggressive.**

Have a look at the following table and the explanations below. Take some time to think about what impact these different types of behaviour have on our communication and relationships.

Passive, assertive and aggressive behaviours

Passive – focus on others' agenda/ others' rights	Assertive – focus on shared agenda/ equal rights	Aggressive – focus on my agenda/my rights
▪ Do not like to express their own opinions	▪ State their opinion or position clearly and directly	▪ Are dominant in group situations
▪ Allow others to take advantage of them	▪ Are prepared to say sorry and admit when they're wrong	▪ Talk/shout others down
▪ Indecisive. Don't commit to action – sit on the fence	▪ Make requests without apologising	▪ Try to get their way in situations
▪ Refrain from complaining when services are below standard	▪ Refuse requests without apologising	▪ Find faults with other people
▪ Frequently make compromises to 'keep the peace'	▪ Give praise where it is due, and accept compliments	▪ Work to personal agenda at the expense of others.
▪ Take direction without questions	▪ Can complain without causing offence	▪ Argue with others
▪ Not standing up for yourself	▪ Fair and reasonable	▪ Believe that others need to be put in their place
▪ Putting others first at your expense	▪ Honest to yourself and others	▪ Pushing your needs at the expense of others
		▪ Opinionated

→

▨ Sitting on the fence ▨ Accept an 'I lose you win' outcome	▨ Look for a 'win/win' outcome	▨ Can be introverted or extroverted ▨ Looking for an 'I win you lose' outcome

Avoid being passive

Passive people focus primarily on other people's agendas and fail to consider their own needs. They therefore find it difficult to make decisions, take responsibility or drive action. They are most likely to agree with someone else than think about their own needs. They abdicate both their rights and responsibilities at work and allow other people's agendas to take precedence/preference.

When we behave passively, we allow other people to make decisions for us and our true feelings are often denied. It is not being honest about your own needs. 'I don't mind' or 'whatever you think' are common replies from a person behaving passively. If complimented, a passive person might reply 'sure it was nothing'.

Avoid being aggressive

The opposite scenario is also evident. In our world of work, where company politics, egos and hierarchies are the order of the day, it becomes clear that there a number of *agendas* at work and generally these are fuelled by personal ambition. What I'm describing here is an aggressive environment which breeds aggressive people. The key feature of an aggressive operator is that they focus primarily on their own priorities and fail to consider other people.

Try being assertive

Neither the passive nor aggressive scenario is ideal. The assertive scenario, however, keeps everyone happy as the focus here is on a shared agenda, that is, both parties in the interaction have equal rights to be heard, and to make decisions. 'I understand your point of view, but I believe …' is a typical assertive response. A person acting assertively can give constructive criticism, complain or disagree, without the other person feeling compromised.

THE ASSERTIVE SCENARIO, HOWEVER, KEEPS EVERYONE HAPPY

passive = your agenda = your rights
aggressive = my agenda = my rights
assertive = shared agenda = equal rights

What you want to do is to minimise your passive and aggressive behaviour and work on your assertive communication skills.

Be assertive

What is assertiveness? The definition tells us that 'assertiveness is about communicating needs, wants, opinions or feelings in a straightforward, honest and appropriate way'. A simpler definition of assertiveness that works equally well is *'being pleasantly direct'*.

Assertiveness is much more than just a way of communicating. It's a way of behaving at work that serves you and your colleagues justly and fairly. And remember, it's not about getting your own way – it's about creating a dynamic where the principles of respect and dignity naturally fit.

Remember in Step 2, we talked about using your influence? I place a great deal of emphasis on assertiveness when I coach people because it's a fundamental tool in using your influence, in a way that is fair and recognises the rights of others to use their influence. Being assertive, and vocalising a need, opinion or feeling that has previously remained unsaid, marks that all-important shift from Concern to Influence. Getting used to using your voice in an assertive manner is both empowering and satisfying.

Joanne's story, outlined below, is a simple but effective example of someone finding their voice and using it assertively.

Joanne's Story: Finding Your Voice

Joanne, a bright and hard-working client of mine, used to complain that her more assertive colleagues got all the credit for work that she had been involved in. Joanne didn't like to be in the spotlight; in fact, she found it pretty torturous to speak at team meetings at all. Her 'solution' was normally to find the quietest spot in the room and to hope no one would ask her a question, and this usually worked. However, she was beginning to notice that her silence at meetings, and her reserved nature in general, was having an impact on her career. Younger, more vocal colleagues, who had joined the company after her, were being given more responsibility and more high-profile jobs whilst she was stuck doing the same thing.

We established that it was important for her to address this growing sense of frustration in a constructive way, not least for her own personal sense of achievement but also her career development prospects. We decided that she needed to draw attention to her very valuable contribution, but in a way that suited her personality. We discussed the options open to her, including scripting and rehearsing her points before meetings but Joanne felt uncomfortable with that, it was too much of a jump for her. We then discussed the possibility of emailing her colleagues with key points prior to key meetings and this sat well with Joanne. She began to highlight her contribution to projects via email and circulated

$\rightarrow$

progress reports to her team in the run-up to important meetings. She also took this opportunity to make suggestions about what to do next.

She immediately noticed a difference. For one, her boss started to acknowledge her hard work and to thank her for her efforts. Her colleagues also sat up and took note. Many of them hadn't really noticed the work that she had put in because she never drew attention to it. Over time, Joanne's opinion was sought much more readily because she used her voice (albeit via email) to highlight her contribution and make suggestions.

Over time, Joanne noticed that opportunities came her way more readily and she found that she was able to create more meaningful and satisfying relationships with her boss and colleagues.

In my experience, much unhappiness at work is caused by the *absence* of assertive behaviour. Either individuals say nothing at all and, like Joanne, see career opportunities disappear into thin air, or people become over-emotional about situations and adopt highly emotional responses such as aggression or bullying.

How to be assertive

Ever had a boss who could persuade you to take on 'just one more job', even when you were totally slammed? A colleague who asked you to cover for them while they skived off? Have you been overlooked for promotion because you didn't ask for more recognition or responsibility?

The two most commonly used assertiveness techniques relate to situations like this, where you find yourself agreeing to something against your own better judgment. Or where unreasonable bosses or colleagues try to impose their agenda on you.

I have worked with clients who are basically doing one and a half times their job simply because they can't say no to a slave-driver boss. And others who have been constantly overlooked because they find it too intimidating to ask their boss for more support or more responsibility.

Making and refusing requests and learning to say no are two of the most common scenarios where assertiveness is necessary.

Have a look at the assertiveness tips and advice below and see if they'll work for you.

Key assertiveness tips

Making requests	Refusing requests
■ You have a right to make your wants known to others.	■ You have a right to say NO!
■ You deny your own importance when you do not ask for what you want.	■ You deny your own importance when you say yes and you really mean no.
■ The best way to get exactly what you want is to ask for it directly.	■ Saying no does not imply that you reject another person; you are simply refusing a request.
■ Indirect ways of asking for what you want may not be understood.	■ When saying no, it's important to be direct, concise and to the point.

$\rightarrow$

■ Asking for what you want is a skill that can be learned. ■ Directly asking for what you want can become a habit with many pleasant rewards.	■ If you really mean to say no, do not be swayed by pleading, begging, cajoling, compliments or other forms of manipulation. ■ You may offer reasons for your refusal, but don't get carried away with numerous excuses. ■ A simple apology is adequate; excessive apologies can be offensive. ■ Demonstrate assertive body language. ■ Saying no is a skill that can be learned. ■ Saying no and not feeling guilty about it can become a habit that can be very growth-enhancing.
Steps in learning to say 'no' ■ Ask yourself, 'Is the request reasonable?' Hedging, hesitating, feeling cornered, and nervousness or tightness in your body are all clues that you want to say no, or that you need more information before deciding to answer.	**Assertive ways of saying 'no'** ■ Basic principles to follow in answers: brevity, clarity, firmness and honesty. ■ Begin your answer with the word 'no' so it is not ambiguous. ■ Make your answer short and to the point. ■ Don't give a long explanation.

▪ Assert your right to ask for more information and for clarification before you answer. ▪ Once you understand the request and decide you do not want to do it, say no firmly and calmly. ▪ Learn to say no without saying, 'I'm sorry, but...'	▪ Be honest, direct and firm. ▪ Don't say, 'I'm sorry, but...'

From www.healthyplace.com

The benefits of assertiveness

Imagine going to work and feeling valued, recognised, powerful and confident.

Assertiveness is so much more than a simple communication technique. It's not something you'll pick up overnight. Becoming more assertive involves practice and discipline. However, the benefits cannot be emphasised enough. Applying these simple techniques can really get you started on a more assertive you.

YOU HAVE A RIGHT TO SAY NO!

ASK YOURSELF...
Do I Need to be More Assertive at Work?

Are there situations at work where you need to be more assertive?

Which of the tips above will work well for you?

Do you find it difficult to ask for support or information from your colleagues when you need it?

Do you find it difficult to be assertive with your boss when s/he makes unreasonable requests of you?

Do you find it difficult to ask for promotion or more responsibility?

Do you consider other people's points of view before putting forward your own?

Do you like to get your own way no matter what?

How can you work more assertively (or maybe less aggressively) with your colleagues?

That brings us to the end of Step 4. You now have an exemplary set of communication and assertiveness tools, that will do wonders in making your working world a happier place.

On to Steps 5 to 7!

Optimism and kindness: a winning combination

05

You can choose to be happy – it's not always an easy choice – but it *is* an option open to you in almost every situation. Did you know that optimists are happier and more successful than pessimists? Being cheerful and upbeat when things are going well for you is the easy part; it's when work becomes mundane or boring – say, when you miss out on a promotion; or when your best friend at work leaves; or when you have to work late for the third week in a row – that having an optimistic outlook will really count. So what is optimism and how does it make you happier?

In this Step, you'll take a good look at how optimism and kindness can work wonders for your work happiness. I want to demonstrate the impact that an optimistic attitude has on

- how you interpret the world around you
- how you make decisions *and*
- your behaviour.

It's quite fascinating to see how the exact same situation is experienced by an optimist versus a pessimist. You'll be given a number of ways to increase your optimism too, from quick-fix remedies to more long-term approaches. And you'll finish Step 5 with a demonstration of how and why kindness and optimism provide a winning combination for a happier you.

Optimism

Optimism simply means focusing on what can go right. Optimists are happier because they expect and anticipate good things to happen to them in their work life and beyond. They also see the best in every situation. So instead of thinking that the nasty boss dumped a load of work on their desk on a Friday evening just to ruin their weekend; they think, 'gosh, aren't I doing well that the boss trusts me with this last-minute deadline'.

The case for optimism is pretty convincing. Optimists are happier, more successful, healthier (physically and psychologically), experience less stress (see Step 8), have better relationships and live longer. Tendencies towards optimism or pessimism are usually in place by your teens but crucially, pessimists can learn to be more optimistic. What this means of course is that optimists can learn to be pessimists too, so beware!

Optimist or pessimist: your way of explaining the world

When we talk about optimism, what we're really referring to is how you explain the world around you. This is what psychologists call your explanatory style. Your explanatory style refers to the way in which you *explain the events that happen in your life, and the meaning you give to that explanation.* A good way to demonstrate how your explanatory style works is to look at the case

OPTIMISM SIMPLY MEANS FOCUSING ON WHAT CAN GO RIGHT

study below. Let's see how two staff members, David and Alan, deal with the exact same situation.

David and Alan: Pessimist vs. Optimist

David and Alan join an Information Technology organisation at the same time. They work in the same team doing essentially the same job. An opportunity for promotion arises and they both decide to go for the new position. A week after the interview, they both find out they have been unsuccessful. David, the pessimist, explains his lack of success in the following way: 'I feel so stupid, I should never have gone for that promotion. I knew I'd never get it, I'd never be good enough to do a job like that.'

Alan, the optimist, explains his lack of success completely differently by saying 'I'm really disappointed not to get the job but John (the successful candidate) really deserved it as he has much more experience than me. I know what I need to do to be successful next time around so once I beef up my experience, I'll have a better chance.'

Here you have two people in exactly the same situation who explained the events and outcome in an entirely different way.

The benefits of an optimistic approach

Your explanatory style is not just relevant to how you explain events. More importantly, it is likely to determine the *decisions and actions* that result from those conclusions.

Back to David and Alan … David, our pessimist, has attributed his failure to secure the promotion to his overall lack of ability and has generalised this event to conclude that he couldn't ever be good enough to do the job, not now and not ever. He says, 'I'd never be good enough to do a job like that.' Chances are David won't be going for another promotion any time soon, as the conclusion he has drawn is that he's not good enough, full stop. In that frame of mind, it's likely that David gets stuck in a rut or ends up in a dead-end job.

Alan, our optimist, has drawn an entirely different conclusion from the same event. He's disappointed about that *specific* interview result but he has a rational explanation for it ('John has much more experience'). Most importantly, he expects to be successful the next time around. He says, 'I now know what I need to do to be successful next time around so once I beef up my experience, I'll have a better chance.' The likelihood is that Alan will go for a promotion at the next available opportunity, and in this frame of mind (and assuming he has the ability of course!), probably at some point in the future, he will be successful in securing that promotion.

An optimistic outlook achieves positive outcomes

Let's recap. In a nutshell, optimists define themselves by their strengths and successes, and because of this they *expect* good things to happen to them. Optimists draw *specific conclusions from specific events,* e.g. 'I did very well in that exam because I studied hard.'

Likely outcome: I am good at exams when I put the work in.

Or: 'I was unsuccessful in that particular interview because there was someone with more experience to fill the role.'

Likely outcome: I'll get more experience under my belt and I'll probably be successful next time around.

Pessimists, on the other hand, define themselves by their weaknesses and failures and therefore don't expect good things to happen to them. This negative interpretation of events leads pessimists to make *generalised conclusions that go far beyond the specific situation* in question, e.g. 'I only did well in that exam because my questions came up.'

Likely outcome: Conclusion is that my exam success is based purely on luck and I'll probably be unlucky next time.

Or: 'I was unsuccessful in that particular interview because I am no good at my job.'

Likely outcome: No point in going for further interviews as I am likely to be unsuccessful in *all* interviews I go for.

It's plain to see from Alan and David's experience that an optimistic attitude sets you up for a happier time at work. We all want to feel hopeful and positive about our time at work. We want to feel that we're not just biding time and waiting for 5pm to arrive. Let's have a further look at some typical optimism and pessimism situations at work and then we'll move on to looking at practical ways of increasing your optimism.

The optimistic and pessimistic viewpoint

The table overleaf outlines a couple of typical work scenarios and presents how optimists and pessimists view exactly the same situation. I want you to think carefully about your own way of explaining things when you go through this table. Are you more of an optimist or a pessimist?

ASK YOURSELF. . .
Are You an Optimist or a Pessimist?

Which column in Table 5.1 do you relate to more?

Which areas of your work life are you optimistic about?

Which areas of your work life are you pessimistic about?

Look around at your colleagues – do you work with happy, optimistic people?

What about your boss? Is s/he an optimist or a pessimist?

Think about the decisions you're likely to make in a positive frame of mind.

Think about the decisions you're likely to make in a negative frame of mind.

What are the likely outcomes of the optimistic and pessimistic views?

Identify three areas of your work where you could be more optimistic.

Look at your own situation

It's really worth putting some time into these questions. Simply acknowledging areas where you could do with being more

Optimism versus pessimism

The pessimistic view	The optimistic view
I'm never going to get through all this work by 5pm.	I'm really going to get stuck in and get through as much as I can by 5pm.
Sarah totally blanked me in the canteen today, she can't stand me.	Sarah was so distracted when I said 'hi' to her in the canteen earlier, she didn't even see me.
There's no point in going for that promotion, Steven is going for it and he's definitely the boss's favourite – I'll never get it.	I'm going to go for that promotion and give it my best shot. Steven probably has a better chance of success, but at least the boss will know I'm ambitious to progress for the next time around.
I bet it's going to be raining on my day off, what a wash out!	I'm going to enjoy my day off, come rain or shine.
There' s no point in telling the boss that I'm being bullied, what do they care? I'll just look stupid.	I need to explain to the boss exactly how I am being bullied, and I'm sure they will be able to help me resolve the situation.
Even after my induction training I can't do my job properly. This is never going to work out for me, I may as well leave now before I'm fired.	Even after my induction training, I'm not sure of everything I need to know to do the job properly, but I'm sure with practice and supervision I'll get there.
I hate my job – why did I make such a bad career choice/ decision? Now I'm stuck here in a dead-end job.	This job is not for me, I need to look at ways in which I can find a new job either within the company or elsewhere.

positive, and making the decision to change your frame of mind, can have far-reaching consequences for your happiness. It might be something as simple as accepting a part of your job that you don't enjoy. So instead of dreading doing the weekly accounts all week and thinking 'I really hate this job', you might say to yourself, 'OK, I'm doing the accounts today. I don't really enjoy it, but it'll only take an hour and then I can forget about it for another week.'

And the million dollar question ... can you learn to be more optimistic? You'll be pleased to hear that all the experts agree the answer is **yes**! Let's look at how ...

How to become more optimistic

In order to become more optimistic, there are two things you need to work on:

1 Close down your pessimism patterns
2 Open up your optimism opportunities.

We'll talk first about closing down your pessimism patterns. Pessimism is personified by negative thinking. Closing down your pessimism patterns means minimising the space you allow for negative thought patterns (remember David? 'I should never have gone for that job') and maximising the space you allow for positive thought patterns (remember Alan? 'I know what I need to do to be successful next time').

Close down your pessimism patterns

Martin Seligman, a renowned expert in optimism, uses the following techniques to get you out of a negative frame of mind in a hurry. These act as 'quick fixes' in moving your thinking from a negative perspective to a positive one.

Have a look at these 'quick fixes'. Think about the times when you are prone to negative thinking and ask yourself which of these techniques would work best for you.

- Remind yourself regularly of things that you have done well and are proud of.
- Activate an internal STOP mechanism. This literally means that you shout STOP to yourself if your thought patterns take a negative turn.
- Practise a positive thinking mantra. In relation to a specific event such as a company presentation, positive thinking works wonders. One veteran motivational speaker I know, who rather inconveniently suffers from stage fright, admits to reciting William Wallace's call to arms from 'Braveheart' to himself before he goes on stage. (Yes, he is Scottish!)
- Stop berating yourself. If you find you berate yourself continually when something goes wrong, commit to accepting and learning from your mistake: 'Yes I shouldn't have got that parking ticket. I know for next time.'
- For the list makers amongst you, writing down the negative thought can have the same effect as airing a grievance – it's out there, as opposed to niggling away in your head.
- Or write down your positive thinking mantra and keep it in your wallet or on your desk. Telephone sales people will often have a

pick-me-up mantra in their line of vision to focus on when a call isn't well received.

- Have a stack of positive thoughts at the ready. Write them down if necessary. You could always have some of these to hand!

Quick fixes are important because optimistic (and pessimistic) thought patterns can turn into fixed ways of thinking. However, a more long-term approach to challenging your pessimistic thought patterns will reap long-term benefits. Let's look at how to make an optimistic outlook a permanent part of your work approach.

Grow your optimism with ABCDE

Based on research carried out by eminent psychologist Albert Ellis, ABCDE is a technique which is used very effectively in optimism training. It takes a specific event and looks at the possibilities for interpreting it in either a positive or negative way. And it looks at the outcomes of either a positive or negative explanation. When you choose to interpret the situation in a negative way, you are asked to challenge yourself to see if your interpretation is valid. If it's not, you are asked to dispute or challenge the explanation and find a more positive alternative.

PRACTISE A POSITIVE THINKING MANTRA

In a nutshell, it's a way of checking that you are not automatically choosing a negative explanation for events when there is a positive option available to you. This is a really useful tool for all of us, for those times when nothing seems to be going our way, or everyone is getting on our nerves. Sometimes, we act before thinking. By using ABCDE, you learn to think before acting. You'll find you make more positive decisions and choices when you step back and look for alternatives.

The ABCDE model

In this model, the Event leads to the Belief which leads to the Consequence and so on ...

A is the Activating Event – a situation that triggers an emotional response. This response may be positive or negative.

B is the Belief – how you interpret the event. This belief may be positive or negative.

C is the Consequence – your behavior that results from your Belief. This behaviour may be positive or negative.

D is for Dispute – challenge the Belief if it is unfounded. Is it overly negative or overly positive?

E is the Effect – Recognise that your belief may by unfounded and by challenging it, you will achieve a positive outcome.

Let's take a look at a real-life example to see how it works.

ABCDE in action

Activating event

The situation
Mary snapped at me this morning when I asked her a perfectly simple question about the report we're both working on.

Beliefs – You can interpret Mary's behaviour either positively or negatively.

Positive belief	Negative belief
Mary has a lot on her plate at the moment.	Mary doesn't like me.

Consequences – How does your belief influence your behaviour?

Positive consequence	Negative consequence
I'll talk to her about the report later when she's less busy.	Mary doesn't like me – I'll steer well clear of her in the future. I'll ignore her next time she needs help.

Dispute – the positive consequence is reasonable. But what is the reason for the negative consequence? Do you need to challenge it?

Positive dispute	Dispute the negative
Nothing to dispute.	Hang on, I've noticed that Mary is behaving the same towards other members of the team; maybe this has nothing to do with me. Maybe she's just too busy at the moment?

Effect – Having challenged the negative belief, you found an alternative explanation for Mary's behaviour, and this leads to a positive outcome.

Positive effect
I'll hold off asking her any further questions until she's less busy.

Think about your own work and how it would benefit from this approach.

Looking back at your own work situation, identify three situations where a positive belief could have provided a better outcome for you.

Optimism versus positive thinking

Optimism is much more than positive thinking. While positive thinking can enhance specific situations, like preparing for a presentation, it does not significantly improve your overall life experience. Optimism, on the other hand, has been shown to enhance both specific and general well-being. So, positive thinking works well as a short-term strategy for *specific* situations, while optimism is a mindset that will improve just about every aspect of your life.

Choose to be happy

Proactively choosing to be happy, and seeing the good in situations, is a much more available option to us than we sometimes realise. Let's face it, most work situations are not black and white, they are rarely all good or all bad. But training or coaching yourself to think 'I am going to find something positive in this situation' yields impressive results. Try it (similarly finding something negative in any given work situation is pretty easy too). In my experience of working with positive people, being optimistic (and happier as a result) is as much a choice and a habit as a natural disposition.

Realistic optimism

To be balanced, it is important to note that optimism is not always the appropriate response. Being overly optimistic may make people overestimate their ability to deal with difficult situations and can be associated with a lack of awareness. You don't have to be happy all the time; happiness and unhappiness are two halves of a whole life. But, while personal setbacks and the problems of the world are all part of the human condition, they don't have to define us. So, while being optimistic is beneficial, it must be accompanied by realism. Making the choice to be optimistic and happy *where possible* is the optimum choice for all.

On that happy note, let's look at how kindness towards others provides you with as much if not more happiness than the person benefiting from your kindness. My aim is to show you just why optimism and kindness are a winning combination. Optimism encourages you to see the best in *situations;* practising kindness encourages you to see the best in *people*. Did you know that practising kindness towards others has proven benefits for your well-being?

In The art of kindness at work (see below), you'll learn that small gestures make a big difference. And there are heaps of simple-to-use suggestions that you can start right away. Armed with a cheerful and generous approach to work, your happiness is guaranteed.

The art of kindness at work
"Kindness is the greatest wisdom."
Anon

The path to a kinder and more altruistic workplace has already been well worn. Philanthropy, community volunteering and charity sponsorship are becoming much more commonplace in the corporate world. Social responsibility has become something of a buzz-word, with a number of high-profile business leaders choosing to use their million (or billion!) pound profits to fund social and educational projects rather than luxury super yachts (think Bill Gates, Warren Buffett and Chuck Feeney).

Involvement in community projects, volunteering, fund-raising, even corporations going green (kind to the environment) are living proof that *giving is good.* There are many and various reasons why these business leaders choose to practise kindness and generosity in this way. However, one thing they all agree on is that it gives them immense satisfacton.

Being kind is good for you

These types of initiatives highlight the benefits of kindness and giving, not just for the receiver but also for the giver. Altruism at work is here to stay and I for one believe that it holds the key to happier work environments and happier employees. So, what is altruism? Defined as 'behaviour that is unselfish and benefits others' it is, put simply, being kind to others. One of the key messages from Step 5 is that a little kindness goes a long way, so lets look at what you can do to make your world of work a kinder one.

You will notice that some of these suggestions have been made in other parts of *Happy at Work*, which demonstrates the natural overlap that exists between many of the core themes. This makes your job of enhancing your work life all the more manageable in that making one small change can impact on a few different areas of your work life.

Here are some ideas to get you started ...

Little and big acts of kindness at work

The little things	The big things
Make someone a cup of tea or coffee without being asked.	Start a mentoring programme (see Step 10) with scheduled meetings.
Greet everyone in your office in the morning and in the evening.	Organise a charity event – see if you can get your company to sponsor it and get your colleagues involved.
Know and use (but don't overuse) people's names.	Start a social club and get people from different departments involved.
Make time for chit-chat. Make sure to include everyone on the team.	Be inclusive of everyone in your office, particularly those who are reserved or quiet.
Organise a social night out.	Support a colleague's career progression.
Introduce yourself to someone new/someone quiet.	Share a new skill with a colleague.
Send a card from the office if someone is out on sick leave.	Be there for your colleagues if they are having a tough time in their personal life.
Smile!	Smile!

Congratulate a colleague on a promotion/an employee award/a good presentation.	Compete with yourself; collaborate with others.
Leave some chocolate or a piece of fruit on your colleague's desk.	Introduce 'kindness' initiatives. Have a 'be kind to your colleagues' day once a quarter. You must do something nice that doesn't cost money.
Wish your colleagues well when they are going on holidays.	Influence upwards to make 'kindness' part of your company culture.
Wish your colleagues well on their birthday.	Write a 'kindness' manifesto for your team/department.
Hold the lift for a colleague.	Volunteer – to go to the shops on a coffee or chocolate run … and to get involved with the company charity.
Hold the door open for a colleague.	Treat people with respect and dignity at all times.
Acknowledge a bereavement even if you are not close to the person.	Get your company involved in local community projects.
Say thank you and mean it.	Say thank you and mean it.

I really like this list – particularly the little things – as some of them are little more than gestures, yet they mean a lot to the people around you. Maybe there are things on the list that aren't your cup of tea or that wouldn't fit your environment.

That's fine, just leave them out. Focus on the things that you *can* apply to your own work situation. How many can you easily apply from the 'little things' list? And if you can pick out three or four of the 'big things' list too, even better for you, and for those around you. Think back to Step 3 and put on your habit-forming hat and off you go …

The following story, told to me on a training course recently, is a good demonstration of how a small act of kindness had large repercussions.

Karen's Story: Kindness in Action

Karen worked in a large public sector organisation that had grown rapidly and become much busier in a short space of time. She complained that the organisation had become very impersonal and how nobody had time for simple niceties any more. An example of this, she said, was that when she went into her office in the morning (a large, open-plan set-up with over 60 people), no one even lifted their head to say good morning. Karen found this very demoralising and it often put her out of sorts at the start of her work day. Many of her colleagues nodded their head in agreement as she told this story.

After some discussion, we came to the conclusion that she and her colleagues could well change this situation in a very simple way; they could simply take the initiative and greet their colleagues by name every morning. Three months later at the next training module, I asked Karen how she had fared. She reported that the simple act of saying 'Good

Morning Mary, Good Morning John' had created a very different atmosphere firstly in her section, and then across the wider department. Having got used to greeting each other in the morning, people began to chat together informally during work, sometimes about work matters, sometimes not. The atmosphere in her section became noticeably friendlier and happier and it became easier and more natural for people to help each other out. People smiled more.

Karen began to greet others in the organisation, those outside her departments, on different floors, in the canteen, and noticed the same knock-on effect. Maybe these improvements weren't entirely due to a simple 'Morning John'. Maybe it was just coincidence that things improved around this time. However, Karen firmly believed that her morning greetings acted as a catalyst for something very positive to take place. And it made a very real difference to Karen and her colleagues' day-to-day happiness.

It's quite incredible to think that simply greeting your colleagues by name could have such an impact. But it's true. A client I worked with recently told me that her biggest issue with her boss was that he didn't use her name when he spoke to her. She found it difficult to get past this seemingly small thing. So, what's the moral of the story? It's worth thinking about the small kindnesses and courtesies that you practise at work. Is there room for improvement?

ASK YOURSELF...
Do You Find Time for Small Niceties?

Do you greet your colleagues every day?

Do you greet them by name?

How do you feel when people don't use your name when they speak to you?

Think about your own work situation, what small act of kindness can you put in place immediately?

That brings us to the end of Step 5. The last two steps have provided you with a thoroughly useful set of skills for managing others in a positive frame of mind. This combination of Assertiveness (from Step 4), Optimism and Kindness (from Step 5) equips you with an enviable set of relationship skills that will carry you happily through your career. Steps 6 and 7 continue the theme of relationships. You will be able to use the skills from Steps 4 and 5, so you'll be pleased to hear you have already done lots of groundwork!

DO YOU GREET YOUR COLLEAGUES EVERY DAY?

Managing your boss

06

Your manager probably impacts more on your work life and satisfaction than you realise. In fact, 50 per cent of your work satisfaction depends on your relationship with your boss, so learning how to make the most of this pivotal relationship deserves lots of attention. The key to any good relationship is openness and communication, so don't forget to use the tips you picked up in Steps 4 and 5.

In Step 6, you're going to work through a number of proven techniques that will help you understand more about your boss and know what's important to him or her. We'll also look at a number of useful ways to influence your boss. This is key to creating and maintaining the best possible relationship. And by the end of Step 6, I want you to feel happy and confident about achieving just that.

What does your manager actually do?

I described the role of management in Step 5 as the art of getting things done, which makes the manager the person responsible for doing just that – *getting things done*. In most cases, the buck stops with your manager: your manager is the

50 PER CENT OF YOUR WORK SATISFACTION DEPENDS ON YOUR RELATIONSHIP WITH YOUR BOSS

first port of call when things go wrong; your manager is the middleman between you and the next level of management and has to try and keep everyone happy. Not an easy task. So, I would suggest that the first thing you need to do is acknowledge that your boss has a difficult job.

The many hats of management

Think about how many hats your manager has to wear: decision-maker; facilitator; people pleaser; adviser; confidant; leader; diplomat; coach; PR genius; barrier/agony aunt; motivator; innovator; disciplinarian; doer; commander … and then there's the day job! So, it's no wonder that they don't always focus on what you feel is important. The key to a productive and positive relationship therefore is to recognise this in your day-to-day dealings with your manager. Remember, you may only make up about 10 per cent of your boss's concerns, and not 100 per cent as we often think.

Let's look at a couple of ways to improve your relationship with your manager.

Ask for feedback

A good way to get closer to your boss is to ask for feedback on a successful project. When the assignment is complete, ask your boss:

- What worked well and what didn't work so well?
- What can I do to improve my performance?

- What could be done differently on the project the next time around?

You can also ask directly about your own performance by saying something like, 'I really enjoyed being involved in that project. Would you be happy for me to be involved the next time around?' This conversation acts as a reminder of your skills, talents and commitment. This discussion serves to cement in your boss's mind what an asset you are to the team. Guess who's in line for the next interesting project?

Failure to provide feedback on people's performance is one of the common mistakes bosses make. Working hard in your job without any recognition or thanks is hugely damaging to morale. We've all been there and it's not nice. So, if your boss doesn't do the feedback conversation of their own accord, make sure to start the conversation yourself.

Arrive with solutions not problems

Before you approach your boss with all the problems associated with a particular project, decide what you can do to solve the problem. Practising your proactivity and optimism habits from Steps 2 and 5 will help you greatly in using your initiative to come up with great ideas, and to trouble-shoot any problems associated with implementing your great idea, so you can't fail to impress and influence your boss.

A good rule of thumb is to avoid any conversation that starts or finishes with 'we have a problem'. Possibly the best way to get on with your boss is to come up with great ideas, and to *solve* problems. Start your conversation with a solution; for example, 'I organised lunch to be delivered from the local restaurant for the boardroom meeting today. The catering manager and two of her team are out sick today so the lunches are running over an hour behind schedule.'

Don't make promises you can't keep

In the grander scheme of things, keeping promises is the 'biggie'. This really sums up everything about trust and credibility, the fundamentals of all your work relationships. Failing to deliver a project or report at the agreed time can be perceived by your boss as incompetence on your part, or worse still that you couldn't be bothered. Realistically manage expectations and stick to your word, even if (and especially if) it is more difficult than you had expected.

For example, if you need to change the deadline, outcome or budget, the sooner you communicate this to your manager, the better. To do this, find the right time and calmly explain the reason behind the changes in the project plan. Suggest to your manager how you can accommodate those changes, what solutions you have come up with, and finally request their support in the new project plan.

AVOID ANY CONVERSATION THAT STARTS OR FINISHES WITH 'WE HAVE A PROBLEM'

Know your boss

Do you remember the Work Motivation Chart from Step 1? The idea behind that was to identify the things that are important to you, especially in relation to your job satisfaction. I want you to carry out a similar exercise in relation to your manager. Understanding what drives your boss's behaviour allows you to read and anticipate different work situations. Getting to know what your boss is going to do, even before they do, helps you decide how best to play a situation. For example, if your boss has a tendency to change things at the last minute and create a lot of stress near a deadline, you might decide to introduce a pre-deadline check to allow sufficient time for changes to be made. In this way, you remove a stressful event for you and your boss, and everyone's a winner!

So where do you get this insider information on your boss? Let's have a more in-depth look at how to read your boss. The Managerial Motives Chart opposite lists key workplace motives and describes how your manager is likely to behave:

  a) If this is an important motive for them
  b) If this is not an important motive for them.

See what the chart tells you about your boss's management style. If you don't know your boss well already, you will get a clearer picture by reading through this chart.

You are most likely to get on well with your boss where you are both motivated by the same things. So building a clear picture of what motivates you (from Step 1), and what motivates your boss, will help you build a better relationship. And the better you get on with your boss, the happier you'll be in your work.

Managerial Motives Chart

Manager's/boss's motivation	If this motive is most important to your manager, they are likely to behave in the following way	If this motive is least important to your manager, they are likely to behave in the following way
Recognition: A culture of openness and feedback, both positive and negative	Your manager will openly acknowledge and recognise good performance. They will probably make it clear to you both your strong points and where your performance needs to improve.	Your manager probably values staff members who are self-motivated and able to get on with their work quietly.
Power: Energised by leading and managing	Keen to succeed herself, she may expect staff to use initiative and maybe even encourage her staff to test the limits and to be competitive. Values independent thinking.	Your manager may promote a more compliant atmosphere and view her own status as more a matter of responsibility than 'being the boss'.
Excitement/Fun: Relaxed work ethic	Your manager will seek out opportunities for having a good time. Enjoys a sociable and relaxed work environment.	Your manager is likely to promote a more sober and work-focused atmosphere among her team.

Altruism: Undertaking work that has a positive impact on other people	Your manager will be interested in your well-being and helpful to others' problems.	Your manager may feel that your personal problems and circumstances should not interfere with work.
Teamwork: Working in a team based environment	Your manager may place a high value on team work and collaboration with others across the organisation.	Your manager may not encourage you to be particularly sociable. May not prioritise friendships on the team or the importance of social outings.
Tolerance / fairness: Motivated by fairness, equity and tolerance.	Your manager will encourage fairness. She may also endorse principled, traditionalist environment and prefer to work within established conventions.	Your manager is likely to promote a pragmatic and tolerant work environment. She may not value methods or techniques simply because they are supported by traditional approaches.
Security: Permanent and pensionable status; low risk role	Your manager prefers staff to work by the book, be thorough and not challenge the status quo.	Your manager may value people who are prepared to take chances and who are flexible and spontaneous in their approach to work.

Money / **Commerce:** Driven by potential to earn a certain level of income	Your manager would prefer staff to be businesslike, direct and focused on the bottom line. She may be driven by the prospect of material success and might strongly approve of profit- making capabilities.	Your manager may give profits and the ideals of an enterprise culture a low priority, and she may not enjoy working with staff whose prime motivation is money.
Culture: Motivated by artistic pursuits and interested in the aesthetics	Your manager may be open to innovative ideas, and is likely to care about the appearance of work products. She would probably encourage an imaginative approach.	She may prefer a practical approach, and would be likely to choose a more routine and structured work environment.
Science / Technology: Adopting a scientific, analytical approach to work	Your manager might encourage staff to learn about new technologies and developments, and would endorse a methodical and systematic approach to issues at work.	Your manager may not be concerned with using a structured framework for decision-making, and she may not consider the careful, logical analysis of problems to be important.

Source: Adapted from the Hogan Motives, Values and Preferences
Inventory (MVPI) and used with kind permission of the UK publishers.

Thinking about your boss's everyday behaviour, identify what you believe to be:

the three most important motives for your boss?

the three least important motives for your boss?

Consider the following ...

Do her motives explain particular patterns of behaviour?

Do her motives explain where you work well with your boss (where your motives are aligned)?

Do they explain where you don't work so well together (where your motives are misaligned)?

How to influence your manager

Once you can tap into *why* your boss manages in a certain way, you can anticipate certain situations and gauge when it's best to approach your boss to ask for a day off (or leave well alone!). People who read managers well do this naturally without even thinking about it. As a result, they tend to navigate their way into jobs they want and work with people they like. You can learn to do this too when you observe and learn from your manager's behaviour.

For example, if you want to have a conversation about your career development, you'll want to think about their Power and Recognition motives. Do they consider career paths important? Do they place a value on giving and receiving feedback? If they don't consider these things important for themselves, they won't necessarily consider them important for you or their team.

If you want to suggest a new idea or a change in policies and procedures, you will want to consider their Tradition and Security motivations. Are they open to change and innovation or do they value consistency and stability? You will find it much easier to influence your manager if you align your work and communication style to their motives.

How will this work for you?

Understanding your manager's motives allows you to read your manager accurately and to anticipate their behaviour. By tapping into your manager's motives, you can decide how and when to use your influence in this important relationship.

Think about a situation that you would like to influence with your boss, and how you will use your insight into their motives in the process.

Jennifer, a Management Consultant, found herself in a difficult situation with a new boss. She tried a number of different strategies for overcoming these problems before finding the right solution. Here's what happened.

Jennifer's Story: Returning from Leave to a New Boss

Jennifer was ten years into a highly successful and fulfilling management career with a management consultancy when

$\rightarrow$

she hit her first career crisis. Jennifer is what's often described as a 'high flier' and had always progressed quickly and without fuss through the organisations she had worked for.

Whilst on maternity leave, Jennifer's boss left the company and was replaced by another senior manager from the business. Jennifer returned early from leave to start work on an important project, and also to make a good impression on her new boss. Unfortunately the move didn't pay off and it became apparent early on that they didn't see eye to eye.

Jennifer's new boss made little effort to integrate her back into the team and continually found fault with her work. Jennifer also found that her new boss had allocated a number of tasks and responsibilities to her while she was on leave that were not part of her job description. She soon found herself struggling to keep up with her workload and putting in long hours, for little or no thanks. Despite numerous promises of support, help never arrived. Added to this, Jennifer found that she had little time to invest in her team, and they picked up on her stress and frustration.

Jennifer found herself becoming more demoralised by the situation and soon gave up asking for support. Added to that, she really didn't agree with the new way in which change was being implemented. It was at this point that she decided to take control of the situation. Life was too short and she had too much to offer to be putting up with a thoroughly unsatisfactory work situation. After all, there were plenty of other companies to work for. She took the bull by the horns, found another job, and handed in her notice. After some discussion with a colleague, an offer was put to Jennifer to remain with the organisation in a different role with a reduced working week, but still reporting to the same boss.

She took this as an opportunity to sit down with her boss and thrash things out. She started by acknowledging their different work approach and she put the following questions to her boss:

- What do you expect of me in this role?
- How can we best work together?
- What are your top three priorities for the next six months?

Instead of feeling that *she* had to resolve every difficulty at work, she handed that job over to her boss. And in handing control back to her boss, she let go of much of the stress and anxiety of her work life. She also decided that she would choose her battles carefully, so instead of continually trying to win her boss round to her way of thinking, she handed the reins back to her boss and allowed *her* to dictate how things were done, even when Jennifer felt she had a better suggestion.

I spoke to Jennifer recently about how things were going. She is back to her old self she said, working hard and getting a great kick out of it. She sticks religiously to her four-day week (but acknowledges that she often does five days' work in four days). She has been able to stabilise her team and to give them the support, direction and attention they craved, whereas she was fire-fighting in her previous position.

And perhaps most importantly, she and her new boss have developed a new-found respect for each other, both in a

$\rightarrow$

professional and latterly a personal capacity. The wariness and resulting mistrust that personified their early relationship has been replaced by an open and honest dialogue, where different ideas and approaches can be expressed and clear expectations set from the outset.

What would Jennifer do differently next time around? First and most importantly,

- Clarify your goals and the goals of the person you report to. You need to understand where your boss is headed, and your boss needs to know you're headed in the same direction.
- Clearly verbalise each other's expectations in relation to those goals.
- Sort out any relationship difficulties, especially with a boss, at the first opportunity. Don't let them fester.
- Keep your overall sense of perspective, especially when times are tough. Maintain your work–life balance especially at this time, so you don't become consumed by the situation, and finally …
- Keep on asking for help, even when it isn't forthcoming. This needs to be done formally, if possible in writing, and in a way that supports the roles, responsibilities and goals of the key stakeholders.

It's interesting to see that Jennifer's first recommendation for working with a new boss (or any boss for that matter) is to understand what their goals are. What are they trying to achieve and what drives them? Once she stopped to think about this and started working with her boss she was able to work successfully and happily with her boss.

This brings us to the end of Step 6. Gaining a more in-depth understanding of your boss and how to influence them is an important part of the quest towards a happier you – and it's good for your career progression too. You'll be continuing with some of the same themes in Step 7, Managing Difficult Relationships, so you have already got a head-start on some of the key tips and tools.

WHAT ARE THEY TRYING TO ACHIEVE AND WHAT DRIVES THEM?

Managing difficult relationships

07

Look around you at work. You will notice that some colleagues move happily through their work life without any fuss. They seem to get on with the job and to get on with others. And it's not that they don't experience the same difficulties as the rest of us, it's just that they don't let these issues become problems. They sort them out in a pretty straightforward way. And then there are those colleagues who are in constant battle with their team, their boss, their world of work, where everything is a problem and reaching a solution takes a monumental effort.

ASK YOURSELF. . .
How Do You Get on with Others?

Which category do you belong to – constantly battling or fitting in nicely?

Which category do your colleagues belong to?

Which category does your boss belong to?

Who's happier?

I want you to think about this carefully because your work satisfaction is determined to a large extent by how you get on with your colleagues.

What's in store for you in Step 7?

I want to wrap up this section on 'Managing Others' by troubleshooting some of the common things that go wrong in work relationships, that is the things that get in the way of your work happiness. We'll explore ways in which to reduce incompatibility with colleagues, such as managing difficult conversations, and bullying behaviour. By the end of Step 7, even the most obnoxious of colleagues will be putty in your hands.

'I don't like you but I can still work with you'

You're not always going to like the people that you work with. The fact of the matter is that some relationships go wrong, or are never right to start with. Dealing with a difficult colleague on a daily basis can be extremely trying and disrupts not only your performance (things always take much longer to get done), but more importantly, your sense of well-being at work. However, not seeing eye to eye with colleagues should not mean that you can't work with them. It just means that you need to learn to manage the relationship in a way that ensures minimum stress for you and them.

EVEN THE MOST OBNOXIOUS OF COLLEAGUES WILL BE PUTTY IN YOUR HANDS

Remember your manners please!

Practising your Assertiveness and Optimism techniques (see Steps 4 and 5) will help your work relationships considerably. I have also found that the best way to deal with difficult people you don't like is to be nice, be professional, be mature, act with respect and dignity, and your counterpart will find it very difficult to be difficult! Richard Templar, in his excellent book, *The Rules of Management*, highlights the impact of this approach, *especially* when dealing with difficult people. 'Even the rudest and most unpleasant person will find it very hard to keep being rude if you are pleasant and open with them.'

Watch and learn

Learning from past experience provides invaluable information. Think about a contentious relationship and ask yourself has your relationship with this person always been difficult? Or have there been times in the past when you worked well together? If so, try re-creating the same circumstances. Can you work on the same type of task or project as before, or work with the same team as before? Even working in the same location as before can make a difference. By re-creating the same circumstances, you may well find you can work towards reproducing more positive results in a happier atmosphere.

If you have never got along with them, are there other members of the team who do? Observe how they interact with the person and copy how they handle the behaviour you find difficult.

We need to talk

Even if you're lucky enough to work with people you like, chances are that from time to time, they will drive you mad. It's astounding how often I hear about day-to-day issues left unaddressed, until minor problems grow into pretty major stressors.

I firmly believe that many of these problems could be avoided by having a simple conversation. And yes, that conversation may be difficult, it may be awkward, it may be downright unpleasant. I assure you that it is far better to have that conversation than to let things fester – because that's when the real problems start.

It's OK to disagree

In order for teams to work effectively, you need to be comfortable having difficult (but non-emotional) conversations with your colleagues. Remember, it's OK to disagree with people, to have an alternative point of view. This is one of the signs of a healthy and mature work relationship. What's important is how you deal with the difference in opinion or approach. Going off in a sulk, ignoring your colleague, or bad-mouthing them behind their back is unprofessional and does you or them no favours. On the other hand, assertively putting forward your point of view, without judging or blaming, paves the way for a pleasant and professional working relationship.

Tackling a Difficult Conversation

An important report is being held up because a colleague has not passed on the necessary information. How do you deal with this? Not by losing your cool, that's for sure. Here is the sequence you should aim for:

■ Clearly present the issue, explaining how it impacts on you. It's important to provide evidence for your difficulty but your manner must be professional and polite. For example, 'Sarah, I am having difficulty completing the quarterly report because I'm missing the data tables which are essential to the summary analysis.'

■ Clearly explain how the person can resolve the issue for you and ask directly for them to do so, outlining your intended outcome. For example, 'You have the information I need to get the report finalised. If we can schedule a 15 minute meeting or telecon today, I can get the report finalised by the end of the week.'

■ Highlight if a real or implied commitment was broken. For example, 'At the meeting three weeks ago, we agreed that you would have the data tables ready by last Friday.'

■ Directly request a mutually agreed commitment to follow through. For example, 'Can we meet later this afternoon or first thing tomorrow morning? Let me know what suits you.'

■ Confirm the commitment and reiterate the key objective of the meeting: 'Great, so we're meeting tomorrow at 9am in the boardroom to go through the data tables.'

> ■ Acknowledge your appreciation for their co-operation and their impact on the end result. For example, 'Thanks for that. I'll be able to make a definite conclusion to the report after our meeting tomorrow, having got your input.'

If you can get into the habit of tackling these types of conversations *as they arise* in your workplace, you will prevent much anxiety and see the positive impact on your relationships in no time.

Bullying – the facts

But what about behaviour that crosses the line? Being patient and keeping your perspective when you are faced with the everyday ups and downs of work is one thing. But there also needs to be a cut-off point, a clear recognition of what is acceptable behaviour and what is not. Let's look at how to deal with more challenging behaviours, such as bullying.

Bullying can be described as 'the systematic abuse of power'. Bullying in the workplace is increasingly being recognised as a serious issue with serious consequences. Research carried out across 70 organisations by Professor Cary Cooper from UMIST reveals that:

■ almost half the survey group (47 per cent) reported they had witnessed bullying in the last five years

- 1 in 10 said they'd been bullied in the last six months
- 1 in 4 said they'd been bullied in the last five years.

The same research found that continued bullying, as well as creating immediate unhappiness, can contribute to long-term problems both in the workplace and beyond. Those who reported being bullied within the last six months consistently reported the poorest health, the lowest work motivation, the highest absenteeism figures as well as the lowest productivity. Based on these shocking findings, he estimated up to half of stress-related illnesses may be caused by people being bullied at work.

What exactly constitutes bullying?

Any negative behaviour that upsets someone else can be construed as bullying. Behaviour that undermines, threatens, deliberately offends or humiliates is bullying. I would always advise a client who thinks they are being bullied to think about the frequency and the duration of the behaviour. It's important, for example, to discriminate between one-off bad behaviour, when someone is under a lot of pressure, and consistent bullying behaviour. There is no hard and fast rule, much depends on the

UP TO HALF OF STRESS-RELATED ILLNESSES MAY BE CAUSED BY PEOPLE BEING BULLIED AT WORK

severity of the bullying (see list below) but regular bullying episodes (once or twice a week), that happen over a 3–6 month period would be construed by most to constitute bullying.

Bullying behaviours

Most companies regard the following list of behaviours as constituting bullying (Chartered Institute of Personnel Development 2007):

- Withholding information that affects other people's jobs
- Humiliating or ridiculing others about their work
- Spreading rumours or gossip
- Ignoring others
- Constantly criticising others
- Invading others' personal space
- Threatening violence
- Physically attacking others
- Making insulting or offensive comments
- Removing the rights or responsibilities of others
- Passing off the work of others as your own.

Being bullied? What to do ...

Protect yourself with support inside and outside of work. Have a few friendly shoulders to cry on whilst you prepare to confront the situation. And whilst this may involve specific training or coaching, it is a critical part of the solution. Failure to confront the bully sends out a message that the behaviour is acceptable, which increases the likelihood that it will happen again. Try to avoid being alone with the offender. If there are other people who have witnessed their behaviour, you may want to talk to them and seek their guidance. Are other people on your team being bullied, or have they been in the past? Can you learn anything from how they resolved the situation?

Meet the bully head-on

The best and most effective method of confronting a bully is to meet the behaviour head-on and early on. You simply say 'Stop, I don't accept that behaviour'. Nipping destructive behaviour in the bud is by far the best option every time. Easier said than done; sometimes it's hard to see bullying behaviour for what it is, particularly if it's carried out as a 'bit of a laugh' but hurtful nonetheless. If you don't catch the behaviour in time or you don't feel that you have the necessary skills to deal with it, maybe you need to get some support from your manager or HR department.

Seek support

Contact your Human Resources department to see if they have a bullying policy and guidelines. They may also be able to provide you with some counselling and support. You will be advised by your HR manager to document the bullying incidences so there is clear evidence available for confronting the situation. This will also help you prepare your script, and you should do this. It's pretty nerve-racking having this conversation, so a script will help you avoid the stuttering and stammering that can go with nerves.

Have the conversation

The next thing you need to do is to arrange a time to speak to the bully. You can do this one–to-one or with a manager or HR executive. I would advise one-to-one if you feel up to it. Deliver your message in a clear and straightforward manner – no frills. Something like:

> Melissa, your behaviour towards me has been unacceptable recently. For example, you undermined my suggestion at the weekly brainstorming session last week, saying my idea was "pie in the sky". I found this very embarrassing in front of my team and the manager. You also rolled your eyes up to heaven on the other three occasions I spoke during the session and this was done very obviously so that the rest of the group would notice. I do not accept that this is an appropriate way to behave towards me and I would like you to stop.

Stand up for yourself

Assertively asking the bully to stop is very important – the message needs to be crystal-clear with no room for confusion.

You can also use the opportunity to ask for an apology or outline a solution, or better still, ask the bully to find a solution. For example, 'You may want some time to think about what I've said so maybe we can meet again next week to look at how we can work together going forward.'

One of the key messages discussed earlier in Step 2 and further in Step 6 will really help you with a bullying situation. That is making the decision to *use your influence*. Facing down a bully is probably one of the more challenging situations that you will influence. It is also incredibly empowering to take on a situation like this and achieve a positive outcome. With the right support and guidance in place, telling a colleague that their behaviour is unacceptable may be easier than you think.

I had a client recently who successfully tackled a bullying situation to great effect. She followed the advice above to the letter. Here's her story.

Susan's Story: Standing up to a Bully

Susan worked as a Sales Manager for an IT training company. Soon after she joined the team, a colleague who had been with the company for many years joined her team from another department. It was her job to train and manage him once he was a fully signed-up member of the team. This fellow, Darren, was very popular and sociable and liked to be the centre of attention.

Soon after he had been trained, he began to undermine Susan, not in a very obvious way to start with, just the odd smart comment here and there. With time, this progressed to his disagreeing with her at every available opportunity and making fun of her in front of the rest of the team. This was all done as if it was a 'great laugh', confirming his reputation as the team joker. Susan's initial reaction was to ignore him but the more she did this, the more obvious and unacceptable his behaviour became. It got to the point where Darren mimicked one of her sales ideas at a meeting with senior managers.

This was the final straw. Not only had she been humiliated in front of other people, but she felt that her career prospects were being compromised if she stood by and did nothing. She made an appointment with the Human Resources department, who confirmed that she was being bullied and gave her advice on how to tackle the situation. The HR manager offered to facilitate the meeting but Susan declined, she wanted to resolve this herself. She arranged a meeting with Darren and outlined that she felt his behaviour was unacceptable, citing a number of recent examples. After protesting that she was 'over-reacting' and it was all a 'joke', Darren walked out of the meeting. The behaviour continued, but in a more diluted fashion; the message was filtering through. It took Susan three meetings to get through to Darren that she would no longer accept his behaviour.

Her perseverance paid off. Darren admitted that he was very deflated about his own career progression. He had been with the company many years but was stuck in a rut and he was taking out his frustration on Susan, whose success he resented. He also wasn't sure he was suited to Sales and was aware he wasn't meeting his targets. His bullying behaviour $\rightarrow$

was designed to deflect attention from his performance. Susan felt that he had potential to develop, so she set up some refresher training for him with one of her best salespeople. She also outlined very clearly for Darren what was acceptable in terms of jokes and pranks and what was unacceptable. Some six months later, Darren had settled into his role and was performing well and his professional relationship with Susan survived and thrived.

A good resource to take note of is the Andrea Adams Trust, a UK charity dedicated solely to tackling workplace bullying: www.andreaadamstrust.org.

Conflict can be good

Conflict at work is not always a bad thing. Some of the most creative and collaborative companies I have worked with use conflict in a very positive way to challenge, probe and problem-solve. These environments acknowledge that there are many potential solutions to everyday issues that arise at work. This allows differences of opinion to be presented in a safe and non-threatening way. Conflict can also be beneficial in protecting teams from 'groupthink' and status quo thinking, which is important for any organisation going through a process of change.

We are all individuals!

And this is where independent thinking or being your own person comes in. It's important to acknowledge and accept the similarities and differences between you and your colleagues. Mainly, it's important to allow and accept that some people think and behave differently to you. Similarly, it's important for you to be your own person. Your work happiness depends on you being true to yourself. Use the learning from Step 1 on Self-awareness to enhance your independent thinking.

In your work relationships, it can be difficult to withstand the inevitable peer pressure that exists in group situations. Bear in mind, however, that your well-being will benefit greatly from trusting your instincts, behaving with integrity, and resisting peer pressure if it makes you compromise yourself.

Stamping your own personality on your work approach and your work relationships can be challenging. But it is an important part of creating a strong and assertive work identity. And a strong and assertive work identity will sustain your happiness in the long run.

YOUR WORK HAPPINESS DEPENDS ON YOU BEING TRUE TO YOURSELF

Be your own person

Some practical tips:

- Treat everyone with respect and dignity.
- Steer clear of office cliques.
- Don't allow yourself to be part of the office bitching brigade (even if you agree with what's being said!).
- Try not to get sucked into office politics – they are full of egos and agendas.
- Avoid the office grapevine – all that grows on it is gossip.
- Listen to your inner dialogue about situations before being swayed by others' viewpoints.
- Stay true to yourself and your values, even if they are at odds with your work environment. There is always room for individuality at work.

That brings us to the end of Section 2 – Managing Others. You have covered a lot of ground in Steps 4 to 7, including communicating assertively and positively with your colleagues (Step 4); being optimistic in your dealings with others, in particular, practising kindness in the workplace (Step 5); and managing your boss, using your influence and giving feedback (Step 6) and dealing with difficult relationships (Step 7). I have found time and time again that by practising these behaviours consistently, you can successfully implement a 'prevention' rather than a 'cure' approach. Preventing unhappiness in your work life leaves the gate open for happiness. Effectively, what you're learning is a set of happiness-sustaining tips and tools to take you through any and every work situation. Use them well.

MANAGING YOUR WORLD OF WORK

Section 03

STEP 8 Detox your work life
STEP 9 Balance your life
STEP 10 Be the best you can be

In Sections 1 and 2 we looked at ways to improve your work happiness by managing *yourself* and your *relationships* in a more positive way. Get these two parts of the equation right and you are 90 per cent there in terms of creating the best work life for YOU.

Section 3 completes the picture with an in-depth look at how you can best manage *your world of work*.

You will learn to make the most of the resources on offer to you through your company, and your wider network. You will also tackle some of the common things that make your world of work more difficult and less happy, namely, stress, work–life balance and detoxing your work environment. You will be following through on core themes from Sections 1 and 2 and looking at how they apply to your world of work.

You'll finish *Happy at Work* by doing some short- to medium-term planning around the ten Steps. This is an important part of creating the happiest career future for you – setting clear goals and striving to maximise your chances of happiness and success.

Let's get going!

Detox your work life

08

Ever find yourself completely frazzled by the Friday evening? Work with someone who is just plain nasty? Or a moan-a-minute? Can you actually see your desk for paper? In Step 8, we'll look at how to tackle all of these scenarios and more. Too much stress is toxic, yet it's an ever-present part of our work life. From toxic people to toxic desks, we'll look at fail-safe ways to reduce stress and keep you fighting fit (and happy!) in mind and body.

What is stress?

Work-related stress is defined as 'the response people may have when presented with work demands and pressures which *challenge their ability to cope'*. Stress occurs in any job and indeed is accepted as almost unavoidable in today's busy world. In reasonable doses, stress can actually enhance performance and can also increase a person's sense of challenge and fulfilment. This, of course, is not the stress that we worry about (if you'll excuse the irony). No, we only worry about stress when we see it having a detrimental impact on our work enjoyment and fulfilment, and this happens when there is *prolonged* exposure to *unreasonable* levels of stress.

There are two types of stress: specific and general, which we'll examine below.

Specific stress

Specific stress is a particular part of your job or a specific relationship. Job-related stress is quite common and is caused by an imbalance between the *demands* placed on an employee to do their job, and the *resources* they have available to them to support those demands. For example, asking a person to prepare a presentation for the senior management team

EVER FIND YOURSELF COMPLETELY FRAZZLED BY THE FRIDAY EVENING?

(demand), when they don't know how to use PowerPoint (resource) may cause significant stress.

General stress

Alternatively, stress can be caused by a more general mismatch between you and the job you do or the career you have chosen. This is why being in the wrong career is so stressful. Some people, by their nature, are more prone to stress, and find everyday situations stressful. Most jobs today are deadline driven, so lack of organisational ability or poor time management can also create a general level of stress.

Keep things in perspective

What happens when you become stressed? Little problems become magnified; small spats become feuds. Molehills become mountains. In other words, stress often causes you to *blow things out of proportion*. And this is where the problems start. Potentially, your relationships suffer, your decision-making suffers, your performance suffers, and perhaps most importantly, your happiness suffers. So it's important to keep things in perspective and nip stress in the bud. Worry not though; we're going to work through a number of solutions to stress in this Step.

Are you stressed?

How do you know you're suffering from stress? It affects you in a number of different ways. First, is the stressful event temporary or permanent? We all get stressed before a big presentation or when submitting a final report to deadline. Generally speaking, exposure to mid- to high-level stress over a six-month period may cause one or more of the following symptoms:

Emotional symptoms

- Loss of confidence in your ability to do your job
- Inability to concentrate or focus on task
- Irritability with colleagues – may become aggressive or angry easily
- Tearful – overly sensitive and emotional
- Unsociable – avoiding contact with others
- Lethargic – loss of emotional energy
- Feelings of loss of control, feeling overwhelmed.

Physical symptoms

- Stress headaches
- Insomnia – poor sleep patterns
- Loss/increase in appetite
- Constantly feeling exhausted
- Breathless – high blood pressure
- Lethargic – loss of energy
- Panic attacks.

Solutions to stress

The following table highlights the most common causes of workplace stress (stress triggers) and provides suggestions on how to resolve these situations. Have a look at the table and see how you can use some of these stress-busting techniques.

The fact of the matter is that we all suffer from stress at some point in our work lives. The key then is to find the right solutions for you to manage your stress effectively.

See which solutions will work best for you.

Meet stress head-on

When I go through the stress triggers in the table with my clients, often their immediate response is: 'What can I do about that?' This might refer to, say, having more independence in your work. My answer is always the same, which is that you can choose to do nothing or you can choose to use your influence. I know which I'd choose. If a lack of independence is causing your stress, for example, you can use your influence with your manager. You might say something like, 'I really appreciate the guidance and support you gave me on the task X, but next time, I'd love the opportunity to do task X from start to finish just to show you what I can achieve on my own.' There are very few managers who could argue with that.

Stress triggers and solutions

Common causes of stress – stress triggers	Suggested solution
Poor work relationships/lack of support from colleagues	Make sure work is allocated fairly. Much stress is caused by thinking you work harder than everyone else. Ensure that there clear channels of communication, and that they are kept open. A major source of stress is feeling left 'out of the loop' or overlooked in some way. Use the range of communication tools outlined in Section 2. Seek a shared interest or common ground with colleagues and use that as a basis for building a relationship. Ask for support from your manager/Human Resources.
Lack of knowledge or skills to do the job	Undertake an academic or professional qualification. Work shadowing/on-the-job training. Up-skill via training.
Increased workload – work overload	Ask a colleague for a dig-out if it's a one-off event. Bring the matter to the attention of the manager – is work being fairly allocated? Delegate responsibility where possible. Learn to say no! Become more organised. Streamline your work procedures.

$\rightarrow$

Poor communication	Take responsibility for your own communication style. You are 100 per cent in charge of how you communicate with others.
	Be clear about reporting lines. Who reports to who? Establish where the breakdown in communication exists.
	Put personality differences to one side – focus on getting the job done.
	Practise assertiveness, optimism and altruism (Steps 4 and 5).
Lack of autonomy/ decision-making	Practise your assertiveness – directly ask your boss for more autonomy.
	Put yourself forward for special projects.
	Bring new ideas and suggestions to your boss.
	Suggest team brainstorming meetings.
Lack of recognition	Ask for feedback from your colleagues and, most importantly, from your boss.
	Suggest de-briefing meetings after each project.
	Suggest team meetings.
	Use the performance review to ask specific questions about your performance and your career prospects.
Personal and family issues	Emotional support from friends and family.
	Seek counselling through your company (some companies provide support in this area) or privately.
	Support from your manager/Human Resources.

Organisational change	Educate yourself as to why the change is happening.
	Anticipate and prepare for the impact the change will have on your job.
	Seek regular updates as to how the change process is going.

Beware the slippery slope ...

It is important to understand how to effectively manage stress because it can have serious consequences. People suffering from stress may become increasingly distressed and irritable. Being unable to relax means that it is more difficult for people to recover while away from work, meaning that they often become tired and run-down. They can have difficulty concentrating and making decisions, and their professional relationships suffer. So that leaves you with reduced job performance and satisfaction. So it really pays to keep an eye on your stress levels and to address the sources of stress at the earliest possible occasion.

Sometimes, the greatest cause of stress is not the job, or the deadlines or the workload, but the people you work with. Not any more! Read on ...

Toxic colleagues

Work should be a positive experience for you, and it should add to your general sense of well-being. But, no matter how much you change yourself, *you can't change others*. And some-times it's the 'others' part of the equation that causes problems.

I strongly encourage you to continue to make the best out of every work relationship by using Assertive Communication (Step 4), Optimism (Step 5) and Influencing in particular, (Steps 2, 5 and 6). Using these approaches creates a natural platform for positive and pleasant interactions, so that your working day is more pleasant. These approaches also act as a natural buffer to a lot of workplace negativity, but…

'It can't be done'

First impressions can be deceptive. Is your colleague unfriendly or just shy? A brash or overbearing colleague may simply need a little attention. So try to see the best in your colleagues and nurture your relationship over time.

However, sometimes, no matter what you say or do, you are bombarded with negative responses. The person you are com-municating with has decided (sometimes subconsciously) that no matter what you suggest, the answer is no, they're not happy with the situation, they can't see the point, it won't work, that's a terrible idea, they're not in favour, they won't do it … and the list goes on.

GLOOMY PROPHECIES SIMPLY BOUNCE OFF A SUNNY ATTITUDE

Optimism rules OK

Just as optimism is contagious, so is pessimism. Positivity is contagious, but so is negativity. So hang around with the naysayers long enough and before long, you may well hear your own voice added to the negative chorus. And this is where Assertive Communication, Optimism and Influencing come in.

Optimism in particular is key to screening out negativity. Why? Because gloomy prophecies simply bounce off a sunny attitude. When you take an upbeat approach in your dealings with others, you naturally create a positive dynamic. So, when you receive constantly negative messages your optimism acts as a shield to deflect the energy-sapping Mr and Ms No!

Protect your happiness

Of course, you can't simply walk away from people you work with. You don't choose your colleagues or your boss. You can try and fix relationships and use your influence to help a colleague to see the world in a more positive light (remember Optimism and Kindness in Step 5). But when you have tried all manner of the above and you are *still* faced with constant negativity, it's time to save your sanity and turn on your toxic filter. Your work happiness is more important than you realise, so it should be protected at all costs.

I am all for constructive dialogue, exchange of ideas, differences in opinion, having full-on disagreements. But you must choose to focus either on the problem or the solution. If you find that some people can't *ever* get past the problem, or when you are consistently told that a problem cannot under any circumstances be fixed, there comes a time when you need to cut and run. And this is how you do just that: you turn on your toxic filter.

How to turn on your 'toxic filter'

- Always remain professional, polite and respectful in your dealings with others.
- Minimise your contact – keep your contact with 'toxics' purely task- or project-focused.
- Keep your head down, do your own work and don't respond **at all** to their moaning.

- Do not encourage camaraderie with 'toxics' outside of your work relationship. Steer clear of the 'how was your weekend?' conversations – this allows the other person to think their negative behaviour is acceptable.
- When pitching new ideas, accept up-front that no alternative is likely to be acceptable to these toxics. Don't take it personally or waste your energy trying to convince them otherwise
- Be assertive about how you conduct your work with this person. Do not present choices and try not to get into long discussions which end up as protracted complaints. For example, you can say something like: 'Sandra, I'll take on the research part of this project and you can do the write-up; there's about the same amount of work in each task, and then next time around we can swap jobs.'
- Anticipate their reservations or objections and have an answer ready. For example, 'Ken, I know you had some reservations about the timescale of this project, so we'll have weekly team updates to make sure we keep on track.'

You may think this is all a bit harsh, but remember **your toxic filter is only used as a last resort.**

When to Cut and Run

One of my favourite jobs is training small groups. I usually deliver personal development or management training, so the courses are very interactive and lots of fun. The reason I enjoy it is that even when you give the same course time and again, you or your group finds something new in the material each time. You get to know people quite well in one day $\rightarrow$

and usually it's a time where people can relax a bit, take time out from the pressure of work, and have some good constructive discussions with their colleagues and a bit of fun doing group exercises.

However, it doesn't always work like that. I have left training courses (thankfully a very small number) feeling like I've been run over by a bus. From the moment I have opened my mouth at 9am to when I have left the training room at 4pm, I have heard nothing except negativity from the group; in other words the day has been toxic.

You might wonder why I can't detox the situation; surely, that's part of my job? Good question. A negative reaction to training can be quite common if people haven't chosen to be on the training course in the first place, and have a pile of urgent work waiting for them on their desk. So, I can understand a bit of bad humour at the start of the day. And sometimes it's good to be able to have a good old moan outside of the office setting, so that's fine too. But, ultimately, once the group has got that off their chest, it's time to move on. People will often thank you for being assertive in combating negativity.

So I ask the group directly for their co-operation, saying something like:

> 'I know some of you don't necessarily want to be here, but now that you are, let's make the most of today. For my part, I will try and make this day as enjoyable and interesting as possible for you. And for your part, I would ask you to work with me and the group to achieve this.

This means taking part in exercises and group discussions, and being open to the information we discuss. And you never know, you might even take away something that's useful to your work if you're open to it.'

This approach, backed up by a solid course usually works, but not always.

Sometimes the toxic people in the group are stronger than me and the rest of the group, and every part of the course is dissected, disputed and ultimately discarded as useless. If the negativity persists after the first break at 11am, I know I'm in trouble. My solution? I put it to the group that I find the dynamic difficult (like swimming against the tide) and again I ask directly for their co-operation saying:

'I'm finding it difficult to work with you if you find fault with everything we discuss without thinking at all about possible solutions. So from now on, for every negative piece of feedback you give, I will be looking for a positive piece of feedback to balance it out.'

This usually gets the right reaction. Nine times out of ten, people get the message and we move on happily. However, on the very rare occasion that a purely negative response persists, I apply the 'three strikes and you're out' rule and I turn on my 'toxic filter'. I simply disengage.

Now, I still deliver the training course but I don't invest any further energy in trying to win over the group or 'sell' the message (which is essentially what training is). I present the information, facilitate the discussion and move on. And I accept that it hasn't been a good day, so I go home, run a hot bath with

$\rightarrow$

lots of lavender and work the day out of my head. Of course, I think about what I could have done differently or better; I try to learn from the experience and the feedback from the group, but I don't take it personally. There was a time when I would have persevered all day to try and get a positive reaction from the group but not any more, my day is too precious for that.

ASK YOURSELF. . .
How Do You Handle 'Toxic' People?

Do you work with anybody 'toxic'?
What impact do they have on you?
What steps can you take *before* you turn on your toxic filter?
What can you do to turn on your toxic filter?
Which tips from the list above will be useful for your situation?

Using your toxic filter is almost therapeutic.

Is your desk depressing you?

Your physical environment has a strong impact on your efficiency as well as your satisfaction, so it's well worth taking

USING YOUR TOXIC FILTER IS ALMOST THERAPEUTIC

a good look around your workspace and identifying what enhances your work day and what doesn't.

Pretend you are walking into your office for the first time: what do you see? An organised and pleasant oasis of calm where you can work peacefully and happily? Or a dishevelled bombsite of a desk filled with old coffee cups and mouldy apple cores? OK, two very extreme examples but you get the point. I am not an expert in Ergonomics (workplace design) but it figures that a clean and clear desk provides you with a much more pleasant environment than one that is full of clutter.

Clutter-free zone please

The clean-desk policy which has been introduced by many companies is a sensible one. Keeping your workspace free from clutter, including stationery paraphernalia as well as last week's sandwich, is not just your manager or company expressing big brother tendencies; it is a well thought through and well researched policy that works wonders for you and your workspace.

Improve your desk life

Some general work environment tips to start:

■ **Noise level** – The ideal location is away from noisy office equipment (e.g. photocopier) and away from the office loudmouth (no, we don't want to hear every phone conversation!).

- **Natural light** – Place yourself as near to natural light as possible, but remember you will need blinds for summer-time glare.
- **Space** – We are not battery chickens although work cubicles can sometimes make you feel that way. With a little creative work redesign (e.g. using under-desk space for storage and filing), you can reclaim a few extra feet of workspace.

And for your desk...

- Look at your available resources (drawers, filing, shelving). Is there a better way for you to organise your desk? Get one of your spatially gifted colleagues to help out.
- Put frequently used stationery and office equipment within easy reach.
- Keep on top of your in-tray and out-tray filing. Set yourself a target of having less than three things in your in-tray at the end of each day.
- Get yourself a personal rubbish bin for under your desk – empty it every day.
- If you eat at your desk, spend two minutes before and after your lunch clearing and cleaning.
- Observe a clean-desk policy if at all possible.
- Having a nice plant or a happy photograph provides a nice focus for the 10 per cent of the time we spend day-dreaming.

Get the Cif out

And it's not just your experience of work that will improve if you adopt a clean-desk policy, your health may benefit from the clean-up too. It's safe to say you probably spend more time at your desk than any other place most weeks. But when was the last time you cleaned it properly? There are some pretty grisly germs about and some scary stories about your telephone handset housing more germs than the toilet seat (yes it's true!). Most people don't clean their desk on a regular basis (usually because there are piles of papers all over it) and the cleaner generally steers clear of it too as it's seen to be your personal space. Plus the fact that many people now eat at their desk so it doubles up as the canteen! So, clear your desk at least once a week and give it a proper clean.

On that ultra hygienic note, we finish Step 8. You're nearly at the finish line. Keep up the good work!

Balance your life

09

Nowadays, managing your *life* can be just as demanding as managing your *job*. What with your family and social commitments, the commute to work, your housekeeping and laundry, not to mention your love life, every minute of the day needs to be planned with military precision.

This Step asks you to think about what is important in your life and how to find time for it. Do you need to adjust your work practice to give time to your out-of-work commitments? If so, we'll look at how to get more balance into your life. And for those of you that can avail of them, the options for flexible working and working from home are also discussed.

Let's start with work–life balance.

What is work–life balance?

It's defined as 'a person's level of control over their work' and it's achieved when you feel satisfied that you are *investing adequate time and energy in both your personal and your professional life.*

The concept and practice of work–life balance therefore has become something of a 'buzz-word' in recent times. A skewed work–life balance is one of the most common sources of work-

MANAGING YOUR *LIFE* CAN BE JUST AS DEMANDING AS MANAGING YOUR *JOB*

place stress. In Step 9, you are provided with a practical set of tools to help you ensure a more positive division between your career and your personal life. According to recent research undertaken by the UK's Department of Trade and Industry, the culture of overwork is more prevalent than ever, with increased pressure on employees to work longer hours under less flexible work schedules.

The Institute of Employment Research in the UK has found that people are becoming increasingly obsessed with their work, by working extended hours, failing to take lunch breaks, and constantly having to compete to progress in their careers.

What's acceptable and what's not?

You may find that many work–life balance issues arise out of too heavy a workload – this is one of the key sources of stress today. However, the odd spate of overwork is not necessarily a bad thing if it's expected as part of the role. For example, those of you employed in accounting or finance roles expect to be busy at the end of month, end of quarter and end of year. People working in magazine publishing have a few really long and hectic days before a magazine goes to press. A promotion at work may mean a finite period of overtime whilst you learn the ropes of the new job. This is an expected and accepted part of the job. It's when an imbalance or work overload becomes a permanent feature of your work life that you may need to take action.

The Five Facets

Let's look at what works well for most people. Table 9.1 opposite outlines the Five Facets of a balanced life, and the key factors that go into each facet. For most people who work full-time, **'Your Job'** takes up about a third of your working week with another third allocated to **'Your Health'** (sleep is included in this facet). So that leaves one third for **'Your Relationships'**, **'Your Hobbies'** and **'Your Community'**.

You won't always have time for all Five Facets and that isn't a problem. For example, the year that you do up your house may be the same year you step down from the Social Club at work. Similarly, taking up a night course may mean that your mid-week night out with your mates is shelved.

The Five Facets of work–life balance

Your Job:	Your Relationships:
Reasonable hours	Quality time by yourself
Reasonable commute	Quality time with your partner
Reasonable workload	Quality time with your family
Reasonable level of pressure or stress	Quality time with your friends
Your Hobbies:	**Your Community:**
Time to pursue personal development – your hobby	Time for involvement in the community – coach local football team
Time for household work/DIY	
Time to relax in your environment – go for a walk – visit a museum – go shopping – sit in your garden	Time for voluntary/charity work
	Time for getting to know your neighbours
	Time for spiritual practice
Time to take your annual holidays	

Your Health (physical and emotional):

Emotionally healthy – general sense of well-being

Adequate sleep

Good diet

Physically fit – exercise three times a week

Avoid any imbalance

The key message from the Five Facet Model is that the first four facets (Your Job, Your Relationships, Your Hobbies and Your Community) feed into and directly impact the fifth facet (Your Health). Too much focus on any one facet leads to an imbalance, and ultimately this will have a poor impact on the Your Health facet (yes, even too much leisure time is bad for you!).

So, in your job, even if you love every working minute, don't mind the long hours, or the weekend work; even if your job is all you want to spend your time doing, it's not a good idea – the other areas of your life will suffer. A consistent work–life *imbalance* causes job dissatisfaction so you'll soon grow tired of your dream job if you work too hard.

Take a holiday

The importance of interests outside of work cannot be overemphasised. People who pursue physical or social activities are *happier* compared to people who do little with their time away from work. Taking holidays has specifically been shown to be important for health and well-being. So the benefits of work–life balance are clear to see. In terms of your well-being and happiness at work, those of you who enjoy down-time or relaxation outside your job are more likely to regain your energy and enthusiasm when you are at work.

What about me?

How can a balance between work and life be achieved? Many of today's policies on work–life balance were introduced to allow people to spend more time with their families but this does not mean that they are only available to parents, guardians or carers. So, what are the easiest ways for you to accomplish a healthy balance between work and leisure time?

Based on research, the following tips have proved successful:

Your practical toolkit for managing your time

- Integrate your personal and work calendar, so you can clearly see your commitments inside and outside of work.
- Keep work time for work only. Keep an eye on how much time you spend surfing the net or on personal calls/email.
- Put your phone on voicemail for an hour each day for uninterrupted work.
- Streamline your work practices as much as possible.
- Learn how to say 'No' when you have a full schedule.
- Resist the urge to compete with colleagues on hours worked, especially if there is a culture of overwork.
- Delegate work to colleagues when you are overloaded.
- Prioritise essential tasks when you are overloaded.
- Use a formal goal-setting approach (see Step 2) to tackling consistent overwork, e.g. set yourself the goal of leaving work on time at least three times a week.

- Get organised. Read *Getting Things Done: the Art of Stress-Free Productivity* by David Allen.
- Take all your holidays – some companies allow you to buy more holidays so do that too if you've had a busy few months.
- Measure your success in the results you achieve, not the hours you have worked.

Tips for life

- Look after your physical health and undertake physical exercise (45 minutes three times a week).
- Make protected time for your family.
- Make plans to see your friends at least once a week.
- Take up a hobby – this can be with friends or family so you kill two birds with the one stone!
- Maintain a healthy diet and sleep regime.

Apart from work overload, your life outside of work will sometimes take over. Being a parent of a young family is, for many people, the time when your work–life balance really comes under the spotlight. And, indeed, it is the time where most people experience significant stress by trying to fit in too much. A long commute has also proved to be a strong incentive for

MEASURE YOUR SUCCESS IN THE RESULTS YOU ACHIEVE, NOT THE HOURS YOU HAVE WORKED

people to reassess their professional lives. With the aid of modern technology there has been a noticeable shift towards more flexible working in recent times.

What is flexible working?

In a nutshell, flexible working allows an employee to fulfil the demands of their full-time contract outside of the five-day 9 to 5 routine. For example, employees can work part or all of their working week from home. They can work three long days and two short days, or maybe start and finish early. Employee legislation introduced in 2006 stipulates that employers must consider *reasonable* requests for flexible working from parents of young children. Other work adjustments outside of flexible full-time work include job sharing and part-time work. Again, employers are moving (albeit slowly) towards a more accepting stance on these working arrangements.

What's your pitch?

If you think flexible working is for you, you'll need to investigate your company's policies to see what's available. The Human Resources Department will have the information you need. Be warned, not all managers or employers will welcome a request for flexible working, so you'll need to do some preparation. Think through the impact flexible working will have on you, your job and your team. Trouble-shoot any potential problems before you approach your boss. You'll need to provide a strong business case. Get working on a personal sales pitch for securing a more flexible schedule. Treat this like you are going for a new job or trying to win new business.

And remember, the arrangement goes both ways, so if you're asking your employer to be more flexible, you need to show them you can be too.

It's not for everyone

Flexible working isn't for everyone. Some people prefer the structure and routine of 9 to 5 and that's fine. Or sometimes, your particular role rules out the opportunity for anything outside this routine. For example, if you work in a role that demands you speak to your counterpart by tele-conference in Glasgow at 5pm local time, you may not be a good candidate for flexible working.

Working from home

The most common and popular form of flexible working is working from home, usually one or two (but sometimes as many as four) days a week. With most homes hooked up to broadband and laptops almost as common as mobile phones, the workplace really has become not just flexible but portable too. Certainly for those with a long commute, or those who want to do the school run, it can really enhance their work life. But whilst many people seem to think that working from home is like a diluted form of real work (think no commute, lunch-time TV, no meetings, and working in your PJs !) it's not everybody's cup of tea.

So have a think about the following before you pack your bags and leave the office.

ASK YOURSELF...
Flexible Working – Is It for You?

The practicalities

Does your role allow you to work out of the office?

Do you have adequate facilities at home (e.g an office space, desk, computer)?

Will your flatmates/family be respectful of your work routine and workspace?

Your preferred work style

Are you a self-starter? You're going to be your own boss working at home, and there are only so many times you can ring the office for advice without losing face.

Are you organised? Can you work to a self-imposed structure?

Are you a good time manager? It doesn't have to be 9 to 5 but must allow you to get through your workload on a daily, weekly and monthly basis.

Can you work alone? You will be spending much of your time on your own and this drives some people crazy. Make sure you break up your day with a trip to the shops or a lunch-hour natter with a friend.

ARE YOU A SELF-STARTER?

Keep up the contact

Research has shown that the greatest resistance to home working comes from middle management, so you need to think about your manager's work style. What are their expectations whilst you're out of the office? How often do you need to communicate with them and update them on your progress? Some managers don't care what hours you do as long as you get the work done. Others will want continual updates and will expect you to be more transparent in your work practice than if you were in the office.

Think about your colleagues too. If they are full-time in the office and you're not, do they think you're at home watching re-runs of *Dallas*? Make sure they know exactly what you're up to with regular email and telephone contact.

Graham, in his late twenties, runs his own company in the film and TV industry. He managed to resolve some of the challenges to his work–life balance and working from home. Even if you don't work from home, his story provides some good ideas of how to create innovative solutions to improve your work situation.

Graham's Story: Juggling Many Balls

Graham runs his own business from home. Working as a casting director for film and TV, his job is to find the best actors for film and TV productions. He does this by running auditions, keeping abreast of new and existing talent, and negotiating deals with actors' agents. Glamorous yes, but also high octane. Graham often finds himself working on a number of different projects simultaneously. His work demands that he liaises with a number of different people including actors, directors, screenwriters, producers and agents. His job, finding the right actor for the job, has to slot into rigid production schedules – so much of the time, he finds himself working against the clock.

Over a five-year period, Graham has built up a successful business and is passionate about his job. Eighteen months ago, he decided to tackle some work issues he had identified as working against his job satisfaction. Below are his top two challenges, the solutions he implemented, and the outcomes achieved.

Challenge No. 1

Graham is a one-man-show covering a multi-faceted brief, so his job can be quite stressful at times. Although he is highly organised, he has to juggle a lot of balls. As well as this, running his own business means that he must look after his own business administration including accounts, business development and day-to-day office management – areas that do not interest him hugely.

Solution

- Graham has taken the plunge and taken on an assistant on a project-by-project basis. His assistant looks after day-to-day administration, leaving Graham more time to concentrate on what he's good at – casting actors.

- Graham has become much more disciplined about how he allocates his time. Naturally organised, his weakness is to

$\rightarrow$

take on too much. He now allocates only 80 per cent of his time, leaving 20 per cent for last-minute contingencies or overruns.

- Using his professional network, he actively seeks out opportunities to collaborate with other casting directors on projects. He has undertaken two such projects recently, both of which have worked very well. Sharing responsibility and accountability makes a job much less stressful.

- Graham has started to outsource specialist functions that he used to undertake himself, such as finance and accounting. Instead of spending his own valuable time doing tasks he finds both time-consuming and unfulfilling, he now gets a professional to do it. This means much less stress and so it's a good investment.

Outcome

- Increased amount of time spent doing the part of his job he enjoys most.

- Enhanced relationships with his collaborators.

- Ability to take on greater workload with the support of an assistant.

Challenge No. 2

Working from a home office can be quite isolating. Graham does most of his business on the phone and by email, so there are times when he can go for a few days without seeing anyone and can end up getting 'cabin fever'. The decision to work from home is financially motivated but he expects his situation to change in the next 12 months. His solutions were designed to act as a stop-gap until he got into an office-share with the right people.

Solution

- Hiring assistant had the double bonus of working in partnership with someone rather than alone.

- Instead of holding auditions in his home studio, he has moved all of his casting sessions to a central location. He also organises all his meetings with producers and directors outside of his office (on average three meetings a week).

- He organises lunch out of the house with a friend on the days he has no meeting, which ensures time away from his home office.

- He checks in by telephone on a daily basis with a close colleague who also works from home. Having a trusted confidant with whom to discuss the trials and tribulations of working for yourself acts as a de-stressor. Remember the mantra: 'a problem shared is a problem halved'.

- He is in the process of going into an office-share in the next three months with colleagues from his industry.

Outcome

- A more varied work life using different locations for auditions and meetings.

- Less exposure to stress (e.g. cabin fever).

- Going into an office-share with contacts from the industy is good for business and good for company.

Graham demonstrated a proactive approach to improving his work life by implementing small but effective initiatives.

Thinking about your own situation, what have you learned from Graham's story? Are there simple steps you can take to make your workday more pleasant?

That brings us to the end of Step 9. So we'll move on to the last step without further ado.

Be the best you can be

10

The last stage in your journey is a busy one! This is where you're going to pull together all the key learning from Steps 1 to 9 to create your own personalised **Ten-Step Action Plan.** This will outline *your* tailor-made solutions for a happier work life, and give you a clear framework for achieving them. But first you're going to look at ways to keep on top of your professional development. Active career development makes you happier and helps your career along too!

Take good care of your professional development

One of the primary sources of career dissatisfaction is the feeling of unfulfilled potential, and this is something I come across consistently with my coaching or career change clients. For most people, a large part of their job satisfaction comes from the ongoing sense of challenge that their role presents, and from the feeling that they are using and developing their skills as they progress through their career. This structured development is known as *up-skilling*.

Keeping on top of your professional development involves adding to your skills-set on a regular basis in line with your career goals and aspirations. Some career paths, such as accountancy, are absolutely clear-cut. For example, they come complete with a range of options readily available for those who want to specialise, generalise or move into management. But other career paths are less well defined, so it's up to you to navigate your professional development.

Go for it!

There are so many good reasons to take on extra learning. It's good for your confidence; expands your skills-set, and it's good for your career prospects, to name but a few. It communicates a message to your boss and colleagues that you are committed to your career. It allows you to actively pursue career opportunities and means that you can demand a bigger pay packet.

It sounds like these are all things to do with your success, but they do make you happier too.

In short, investing in your personal and professional development is good for *you* and your *career satisfaction and success.*

Maybe you're not sure you're up to further training. Well, you can choose to study at any level, so there will always be a good starting point. Why not try a night course to dip your toe in the water? Why not try it and prove to yourself you can do it?

Maybe you're not sure that you want to stay in the same career? Maybe you don't have a solid career plan? So, it's hard to know which course to do. Or if you should bother at all? My advice is – do it. Sometimes, a clearer sense of direction comes from a work-enhancing initiative, and not the other way around. In other words, maybe by training and investing in yourself, you will find a natural path or direction emerging. Remember your internal career compass from Step 1?

The three-year itch

A good rule of thumb is to add something new to your skills-set every two to three years, so that you are continually learning and growing. If it's work related, well and good, but it needn't be. I worked on a staff development project with a great company in London who were very big on investing in their people. Once you were in the company three years, you had to go on a training course of your choice, paid for by the company. The only stipulation was, it could *not* be work related. Inspired! (Incidentally, it was also the 'happiest' company I have ever worked with.) Non-work related training or up-skilling is great for you too.

Let's look at some of the options open to you.

Up-skilling: the options

There are two main routes to up-skilling – first, via in-house training courses run by your company, and second through external training which may be sponsored by your company. We'll talk first about the in-house opportunities:

In-house training

Companies have become much more proactive in how they manage career development, and you may have a formal training allowance (say four days a year) built into your contract. Research has shown that 'learning organisations' (those organisations that place a strong emphasis on training and development and back this up with specific resources) retain staff longer and have a higher level of staff morale than non-learning organisations (those with no formal training and development policies). I often advise clients who find it (more) difficult to manage their own career development to target 'learning organisations' who will do this job for them.

Continuing Professional Development – what's that?

Within the majority of career areas, there is an increasing emphasis on Continuing Professional Development (CPD), and many professional bodies now insist that you undertake regular accredited training which is noted on a CPD log. Within companies, Personal Development Plans (PDPs), where you chart out how you would like your career to develop, have become an integral part of the (performance) review process (your 6 or 12 monthly chat with your manager about how your job is going). Learning and Training usually form part of or are aligned to the Human Resources (HR) department of your company, so get in touch with your Training Officer or HR and see what's on offer.

External training and further study

The first port of call in up-skilling is to identify the right training course or qualification for you. Get in touch with the professional body that represents your career sector or industry. Making sure your course is recognised or accredited by the professional body is rule number one, so getting a careers pack from them should be first on your agenda. This information can generally be accessed on the internet too. Your careers pack will list all the entry routes into the different parts of your industry and tell you what you need to do to get there. It will list the range of training options available from educational, professional, vocational and on-the-job training.

Second, you need to think about the type of course that suits your learning style. The options for up-skilling are numerous, ranging from formal educational and professional qualifications (through universities and colleges of further education plus through the professional body itself) to less formalised learning through seminars, lectures and workshops. Then there is vocational and on-the job training, which emphasises the practical skills you need to progress in your job.

The options are endless

The availability of further training and development courses has vastly increased with the options of studying full-time, part-time, by distance learning or e-learning available to all. If you're new to the training or further study game, or if you haven't studied in a long time, you might also want to consider a night course just to test the water. Access to further training and study has also opened up more and more opportunities for mature students and those with little or no formal educational background. So, there's no excuse. If you want to keep yourself motivated and challenged in your job, and if you want to ensure your job satisfaction stays buoyant, get into the training room or studying; www.learndirect.co.uk is a fantastic resource for accessing information on all types of courses and qualifications.

Listen and learn

Is there someone at work who inspires you – whose work style or way of communicating is always impressive?

Increasing your skills-set doesn't just happen formally in the training room or in the classroom. Lots of learning happens on the job, without you even realising it. Through observing and learning from your colleagues and your bosses, you find yourself naturally willing and able to take on more responsibility, make better suggestions and decisions, and grow in confidence. This natural mentoring or coaching dynamic has been found to be extremely powerful in enhancing a person's experience of work, both on a performance and on a satisfaction level. It has resulted in the development of formal coaching and mentoring programmes which have become an accepted part of the work environment.

Mentoring versus coaching?

The terms 'mentoring' and 'coaching' mean different things to different people and often the terms are used interchangeably. However, there are a number of important distinctions and it's important to recognise those distinctions so you can consider which is the best method for you.

Mentoring describes the process whereby a more senior and experienced member of staff assists you in developing your *general* skills and ability for a role. A mentor often tells you what to do or tells you what they would do in a certain situation. It is often offered to those who have been earmarked for promotion to help them prepare for increased responsibility.

Mentoring happens partly by discussion and partly by demonstration (e.g. you may sit in on a management meeting with your mentor and observe how they behave). Coaching, on the other hand, is used to help individuals address a *specific* work task or work relationship such as how to provide feedback to team members.

Coaching is usually facilitated by an external consultant who is a qualified Business or Executive Coach. Coaching happens mainly by discussion –a coach and his/her clients are equal partners. Coaches do not give advice; instead, they prefer to act as a catalyst in helping you to diagnose the issue and work towards a specific outcome yourself.

The benefits of coaching and mentoring programmes

- To help you learn and develop your technical and interpersonal skills.
- To help you clarify and achieve your career goals.
- To enable you to find new ways to solve old problems.
- To provide a sounding board for your ideas and aspirations.
- To demonstrate your company's commitment to you.

What's in it for you?

And how does this make you happier? Much like the training and development, it keeps your career development on track. It helps you to constructively address workplace challenges as they arise and achieve a positive outcome; and it facilitates goal-driven behaviour. All three of these things (career development, overcoming challenges, and goal-setting) are integral to job satisfaction. The message is clear therefore: avail yourself of any mentoring or coaching opportunities that come your way. Or better still, put yourself forward as a candidate to your manager, and you are on the road to a happier you.

Short- and medium-term career planning

This is a good opportunity to remind yourself of the benefits of goal-setting (Step 3). The SMART framework in particular is great for plotting what you want your career progression to look like. People who set regular career goals experience more job satisfaction. This is partly to do with opportunities related to extra training, but also to do with the sense of accomplishment and fulfilment that results from being in control of your career destiny.

So, it plays an important role in increasing your job satisfaction as well as propelling your career forward.

Tamsin's story

Tamsin left university after two years to join a large retail bank. She was studying for a degree in Modern Languages. She now works as an Adminstrator and would like to get into the International Division. She has recently been offered a place to complete her degree by night (part-time) study at her old university. What does she need to think about before she accepts? Let's look at how Tamsin used the SMART framework to map out her goal.

By planning her goals and using the SMART framework to map it out, Tamsin can clearly see the ups and downs of her journey ahead. Ask yourself:

- Can you see how the SMART framework will keep her on track?
- How exactly will it help her achieve her goal?
- What about your own training?
- Would SMART make is easier for you to up-skill?

Using the SMART template for medium-term career planning (1–3 years)

TAMSIN'S MEDIUM-TERM GOAL IS TO COMPLETE AN HONOURS DEGREE IN THE NEXT THREE YEARS	
Identify and write down your goal	I would like to complete my degree in Languages with Honours in the next three years.
Is your goal SMART?	**Specific:** Yes – complete my degree
	Measurable: Yes – by night and whilst continuing my full-time job
	Achievable: Yes – if I study hard!
	Results Oriented: Yes – I want to get Honours
	Time-bound: Yes – in the next three years
What are the key milestones to achieving your goal?	I have two years completed of a three-year course. It will take me at least another two years to complete it on a part-time basis. The key milestones will be my annual exams plus the completion of my final year thesis.

Identify support/resources available to you to achieve your goal	My manager has said that he will pay half my course fees from the Learning and Development budget, on the basis that I am successful in passing my exams.
	I am entitled to study leave for one week before exams.
	My cousin completed her degree in Languages last year and has offered to tutor me and give me her books plus lots of essays too!
	My Mum has offered me my old room for me to study at weekends. I share with four others and the house is busy, especially at weekends, so not very study-friendly.
	The college I have enrolled in also offers extra tutoring to returner-learners so I will definitely avail myself of that in the first year anyway.
Identify any potential obstacles to achieving your goal	Work has been really busy of late and I have ended up bringing work home with me a few times in the last three months. I will have to make sure this doesn't happen any more. I will need to talk to my boss and team to gain their support in this.
	My house-share is not really conducive to studying so I'm going to stay with my Mum in the run-up to and during exams as well as studying there at weekends.

$\rightarrow$

	Work is going to pay half of my fees but that still leaves me with £2,000 to pay over two years so I'll have to cut back on my outgoings, as well as get a bank loan.
Re-visit, review and refine your goal (in light of resources available and obstacles present)	My goal is still on track – I've been quite conservative giving myself three years to complete a two-year course, so hopefully I can deal with any contingencies.
Track your progress – carry out a three-monthly review	To do as I go along. I have put tracking dates into my personal and work calendar to highlight exam and thesis submission dates. I have also put in essay submission dates and exam preparation timetable, so hopefully I have all bases covered.
Measure your outcome against your initial goal	Ask me again in three years!
Measure your outcome against your revised goal	

Your very own unique and personalised Ten-step Action Plan

OK, time to stop reading and start doing! Well done for getting this far. Your pursuit of a happier work life will be helped considerably by creating your own personal Action Plan. This will prepare you in a concrete way for putting some new 'happiness habits' into practice.

Think about the amount of time you spend surfing the net every day, or researching your next holiday, and compare that to the amount of time you spend monitoring and evaluating your career satisfaction and happiness. Think of how many self-improvement books like this you read, but don't quite get around to applying the learning – we've all been there.

So, *right now,* before you put down the book and think, 'hmm interesting ...', I want you to flick back through each Step and think about which part of the Step resonates with you. Was there a particular point that made perfect sense to you? That seemed to describe your situation exactly? Was there a question that struck a chord with you?

Over to you

I want you to take *one* and *only one* piece of learning from each Step and fill out your own Action Plan in as much detail as you can (you can schedule this part into your diary if you *really* don't have time right now). Remember, this is about your work satisfaction and happiness, and not career success or progression. Use the following table as your template.

Just to give you a head start, I asked one of my clients, Phil, to do a trial run and fill out Steps 1, 4 and 8 (the first Steps from each Section) for the Action Plan.

Phil, mid-thirties, is a Graphic Designer with a large advertising agency. He has worked in that role for the last 18 months and loves it. He would like to go for the job as Lead Designer, managing the team of four Designers, but has never managed people before – his role has always been stand-alone.

This is what he came up with ...

Ten-step Action Plan

Step	Key message for me from this Step	Specific issue
SECTION 1 MANAGING YOURSELF		
Step 1 **Self-awareness**	I found the job satisfaction cycle really interesting.	I have a low boredom threshold, so looking back over my work over the last ten year see that my satisfacti peaks after two years but dips if I stay in th same job any longer than three years – scary! I'm really happy whe work right now and would like to stay he for at least another three years.
Step 2 **Motives and Values**		
Step 3 **Goals**		

sired action/ tcome	How?	Timescale
ake an internal move, eferably a promotion, the next year before tart getting itchy feet.	OK, so I know I will probably be bored in about a year's time, so I'd better think ahead. I'm going to put myself forward for the in-house mentoring programme, so the boss knows I'm keen to progress. And I'm also going to undertake a Management Diploma so I can learn the tools of the management trade. I will also sound my boss out at review time to see when there may be a vacancy arising at Lead Design level.	Mentoring programme starts in January. Diploma in Management starts next month. I will schedule a meeting with my boss before my review in December – that's four months away and I need to get a clear idea of opportunities sooner than that.

$\rightarrow$

SECTION 2 MANAGING OTHERS

Step 4 Communication	It was hard to pinpoint just one thing as there were so many things in the communications piece that I could identify with. If I had to choose just one, definitely the case study where Joanne managed to 'find her voice'. That's me!	I have often felt exactl the same as Joanne! Working in an Ad agency, there are so many loud and asserti people vying for attention. I am a 'quiet creative' but very goo at what I do. I sometimes come out meetings nearly crying because other people have talked over me o not listened to what I have to say, even though I had great ide
Step 5 Optimism		
Step 6 Managing Your Boss		
Step 7 Managing Difficult Situations		

eed to find a way to ake my voice heard d I want to learn to mmunicate sertively, particularly if m going for a omotion in the next ar.	I think preparing a script for important meetings is a great idea, I know it'll seem weird rehearsing for a meeting, but if it means I can get my point across, it's worth it. It will also get me noticed by senior managers. I need to show that I can be assertive enough to lead a team. I think I will still find it challenging to avoid being interrupted so I am going to have to learn to stand my ground when this happens. Even saying something simple like 'sorry Stephen, but I wasn't finished speaking' seems more possible to me now.	No reason why I can't put this into practice immediately. No time like the present! To do: Prepare and practise script for the next team meeting.

$\rightarrow$

SECTION 3 MANAGING YOUR WORLD OF WORK		
Step 8 **Stress Management**	The point about workload and stress really hit home for me. I could identify with all the symptoms of stress – aaaggghh!	Working as a Designe attention to detail is critical, and I am the first to admit that I ar a perfectionist. I work to daily deadlines anc often find that I can't finish pieces to the standard I'd like. I get really stressed if I hav to send out work tha feel could be better.
Step 9 **Work–Life Balance**		
Step 10 **Opportunities**		

vould love less stress my day (who ouldn't?) but *not* at e expense of my ork. I want to send t work that I'm really oud of. I'm good at nat I do and I deserve enjoy my success stead of feeling essed all the time. nd maybe, in general, like to chill out a le and try and go a easier on myself nen my perfectionist ndencies are really king in.	My work is always very well received by my Manager and the client so I need to consciously listen to that feedback and be happy with what I've produced and achieved – instead of feeling stressed about what I didn't have time to do. I also need to learn to delegate, I can pass on preliminary work to the junior designers. And I'll be making a lot more use of the interns going forward.	Again, this is one I can put into practice right away. I just need to get into the habit of delegating part of every project. I'm sure I'll soon get used to it!

$\rightarrow$

Now it's your turn. Try and complete the Ten-Step Action Plan in one sitting, with no distractions, and you'll find that you really get into the swing of things. You will be setting yourself some timelines for putting your ten steps into action – if you have too many simultaneous deadlines, you may need to give yourself a bit more time here and there.

Enter your deadlines in your diary and your Outlook and revisit your Action Plan every three months. Go easy on yourself if you don't get it all right first time – the important thing is to move in the right direction. Making even the smallest change to your work life makes a big difference to your happiness.

That brings you to the end of your ten-step journey – well done!

Happy Working ☺

MAKING EVEN THE SMALLEST CHANGE TO YOUR WORK LIFE MAKES A BIG DIFFERENCE TO YOUR HAPPINESS